Columbia University

Contributions to Education

Teachers College Series

No. 468

AMS PRESS
NEW YORK

THE BEARING OF CERTAIN PERSONALITY FACTORS OTHER THAN INTELLIGENCE ON ACADEMIC SUCCESS

A STUDY OF TESTS MADE AT TEACHERS COLLEGE, COLUMBIA UNIVERSITY

BY

HENRY T. TYLER, PH.D.

TEACHERS COLLEGE, COLUMBIA UNIVERSITY
CONTRIBUTIONS TO EDUCATION, NO. 468

BUREAU OF PUBLICATIONS
Teachers College, Columbia University
NEW YORK CITY
1931

Library of Congress Cataloging in Publication Data

Tyler, Henry Teller, 1900–
  The bearing of certain personality factors other
than intelligence on academic success.

  Reprint of the 1931 ed., issued in series: Teachers
College, Columbia University. Contributions to
education, no. 468.
  Originally presented as the author's thesis, Columbia.
  Bibliography: . p.
  1. Character tests. 2. Personality. 3. Grading
and marking (Students) 4. Columbia University.
Teachers College––Students. I. Title. II. Series:
Columbia University. Teachers College. Contributions
to education, no. 468.

LB1131.T9 1972   378.1'6'62   78-177693
ISBN 0-404-55468-7

Reprinted by Special Arrangement with Teachers
College Press, New York, New York

From the edition of 1931, New York
First AMS edition published in 1972
Manufactured in the United States

AMS PRESS, INC.
NEW YORK, N. Y.   10003

ACKNOWLEDGMENTS

Grateful appreciation is expressed by the writer to Professors Goodwin B. Watson, Rudolf Pintner, Ralph B. Spence, and Percival M. Symonds, who, as his dissertation committee, gave many valuable suggestions and never-failing encouragement; to Dr. Laura B. M. Krieger and her assistants, who did much of the preliminary scoring and gathering of supplementary data; to Mrs. Emma T. Tyler, his mother, and Wilfred W. Tyler, his wife, who rendered long hours of invaluable labor in tabulation and other equally fascinating occupations incident to the preparation of this monograph.

H. T. T.

CONTENTS

TABLES

CHAPTER I

STATEMENT OF THE PROBLEM

Although the attempt of scientific measurement to hew a path through that intricately tangled jungle which we call human personality has as yet succeeded in penetrating but a few feet, already a large number of persons have bent their best efforts toward the ultimate success of the tremendous undertaking. Volumes have been written, both from the deductive point of view of the interested spectator and from the experimental point of view of the active laborer, to enable man to understand what he has been wont to call his "self." Battles have raged, are raging, and shall doubtless continue to rage for some time between staunch defenders of diverse systems of attempted explanation.

As one surveys the present status of the undertaking, he is impressed with the insignificance of the progress, the immensity and density of the jungle of ignorance yet remaining to be conquered. Men have made but a bare beginning toward understanding the laws which govern the development and continuity of that which is called the self, or the elements which go to compose it. And as for ways of measuring the total self, or even its elements, they can scarcely be said yet to have begun at all.

In spite of this, man continues to live, although nearly every moment of life involves some interaction between a person, or "self," and one or more other persons, or "selves," any one of which interactions may be fraught with the gravest of consequences for at least one of the "selves." Illustrations of this might be taken from any phase of life; but not to prolong the discussion, and to come to the immediate problem, we may consider the interaction between "selves" which follows when an individual seeks admission to a teacher training institution. Obviously, not all applicants are equally fitted to profit by the training there available, nor to become acceptable teachers after such training. For some of these "applicant-selves," then, acceptance will mean one or more years of relatively unfruitful effort, resulting finally in failure or mediocrity. For others, rejection will be an equally tragic mistake, for they possess the qualities necessary to successful effort in the institution and beyond.

In recent years many institutions of higher learning have had more applicants for admission than they could accept. How shall the academic sheep be separated from the goats? Shall those whose high school records are above a certain average be the only ones accepted? But evidence piles up that good work in the secondary school gives no assurance of equally good work in the college or normal school. Shall those who make the best scores on intelligence tests be accepted, the rest rejected? Again there is ample evidence to show that intelligence alone does not guarantee successful class work in such subjects as comprise the usual undergraduate curriculum. Can other significant factors be found, the presence or absence of which in an individual bears an important relation to the quality of academic work that he will most probably do? If such factors can be found and measured in a convenient manner, it would be desirable to add them to measures of intelligence and high school record when attempting to select for admission to higher education those best able to profit from it.

The statistical approach to the problem of predicting academic success involves the giving of certain tests to prospective students and the application of a previously developed formula, called a regression equation, to the test results. From this the average class mark which the prospective student will most probably make is secured, together with a statement of the upper and lower limits within which his mark will almost certainly fall. If the prediction is crude, this range from upper to lower limits may be nearly as great as the range of average marks of all the students; if enough factors of the right sort are measured, so that the prediction is very accurate, the range will be small.

The accuracy of the predictions when compared with the average of marks actually obtained is expressed by means of the coefficient of correlation, r. Were the prediction no better than blind guesswork, this coefficient would be approximately zero, .oo. Were the prediction perfect, coinciding exactly with the average marks secured, the coefficient would be one, 1.oo. Thus, as r approaches 1.oo in size, it indicates increasing accuracy of prediction.

When predictions of academic success in college in terms of average class marks are made on the basis of intelligence test scores alone, the predictions are by no means perfect. A great many such studies have been made yielding coefficients of correlation ranging from nearly zero to .8o. The average, obtained from an extensive summary of these studies, is found by Krieger [48] * to be from .43 to .48. That is, the correlation between intelligence and class marks at the college level is in the neighborhood of .45.

Naturally, in predicting achievement or aptitude of whatever sort, we do not expect perfect accuracy. Too great a variety of relatively independent factors operates to determine success in any field of human endeavor which we may be studying. But we do desire that our predictions be accurate enough to be of real value in discriminating, in the case of the present problem, between individuals who may be expected to do good academic work and individuals who are unlikely to do acceptable academic work. How accurate need our predictions be to have practical value?

Hull [40 : 276] gives the following table for interpreting the value of a coefficient of correlation obtained between a series of predicted measures and the measures actually secured:

> Below .45 or .50, practically useless for differential prognosis.
> From .50 to .60, of some value.
> From .60 to .70, of considerable value.
> From .70 to .80, of decided value but rarely found.
> Above .80, not obtained by present methods.

He assumes here that the coefficients have been corrected for attenuation due to errors of measurement. Were they uncorrected, they would be lower throughout.

The usually obtained coefficient of about .45 between intelligence and college marks indicates that so long as we attempt to predict marks from intelligence alone, our predictions are of little real value. Some students whose intelligence scores are unfavorable will, if given opportunity, make very satisfactory marks; and others with high intelligence will make mediocre or even unacceptable marks. The error of prediction is altogether too great.

What are some of the other factors which may be thought to play an important part in determining one's scholastic success? Out of a vast number of possible factors there may be mentioned health, amount of work carried outside of college,[1] academic load carried, interest in school work, and emotional adjustment. Each of these

---

* Numbers in brackets refer to bibliographical references, pages 85–89. A second figure following a colon indicates the page referred to.

[1] An unpublished study by Anderson (Anderson, Roy N., "An Investigation of Students at Teachers College with Respect to Their Wage-Earning Activities and the Relation Between These and Various Aspects of Their University Work," 1929), made on the same students from whom the data of the present study were obtained, indicates that with intelligence constant there is no relationship between number of working hours and academic marks ($r = +.02 \pm .03$; $N = 422$).

may be thought of as a complex set of factors, some of more importance than others, and as dynamic rather than static in any given person. Only as they are analyzed, measured, and their varying amounts of influence on marks noted, can we improve markedly our ability to develop test batteries by means of which academic aptitude may be satisfactorily predicted.

We may think of this problem of predicting academic success as analogous to the chemist's problem of analyzing a very complex compound.   He must make both a qualitative and a quantitative analysis before he can produce the compound in his laboratory.   So, before we can become able to predict with satisfactory accuracy the academic success of any student, we must complete at least the major parts of our qualitative analysis (that is, we must discover just what factors play a significant part) and of our quantitative analysis (that is, we must know just how much or how little of any factor makes it a significant one).   When we remember that our material, unlike the chemist's, is constantly changing even as we try to analyze it, it will be apparent that the ultimate solution of the problem lies a long distance ahead.   Yet some progress may be made, and may be enough to be of considerable practical value.

The phase of this large problem which is to be dealt with here is that of the relationships existing between academic success in normal school work as measured by the average of first semester marks, and the probable emotional adjustment of the student.   Specifically, the task is to study a particular technique for measuring a variety of factors thought to indicate emotional disturbance, and to determine the value of this technique as a predictive instrument when used in conjunction with measures of intelligence.   How much, by the use of this method, can the coefficient of multiple correlation between actual and predicted marks be raised?   The technique to be investigated, the Self-Ordinary-Ideal Rating Scale, will be described in the third chapter.   First, however, the results of certain previously reported studies which attempt to predict academic success at the college or normal school level will be reviewed briefly.

CHAPTER II

VARIOUS APPROACHES TO THE PREDICTION OF ACADEMIC SUCCESS

That human personality is the resultant of the interplay of a great number of more or less independent factors is obviously true. Of these, intelligence is only one, or perhaps more truly, is but one aggregate or system of related factors. In general, this aggregate may be said to be largely determined by the particular quality of the physiological make-up of any given individual. The degree of sensitivity of one's nervous system, determined by his heredity, sets the upper limit of ability, which environment, however favorable, may not transcend. It is this degree of sensitivity, or to state it in terms of outcome, of adaptability or capacity for adjustment, which our present-day intelligence tests measure with more or less success. Though none is perfect, these measures are of sufficient accuracy, in the main, to be of material assistance in school administration, personnel guidance, psychiatry—in short, in any situation which demands a working knowledge of any person's intellectual equipment.

That intelligence is only one of the factors which go to make up success or failure—be it in business, in home relationships, or in academic life—is not only a common sense observation, but one which is abundantly borne out by experimental evidence. To those who for one reason or other have need to be able to predict with considerable accuracy what sort of adjustment a given person will make to a certain kind of environment, the results yielded by intelligence tests alone are highly unsatisfactory. In the field of school administration, which is the immediate concern of this study, many attempts have been made to find intelligence tests or batteries of intelligence tests which would give results of satisfactory predictive value of school achievement. As representative of these there may be mentioned Fretwell's [20], one of the earlier studies; that of Rogers [67], describing the use of the Thorndike Intelligence Examination at Goucher; Burwell and MacPhail's [9] report of testing at Brown University; Anderson and Spencer's [3] studies in testing at Yale; and

Johnston's [41, 42] work at the University of Minnesota.   Indeed, few are the colleges or normal schools in which attempts are not being made to-day to select in advance students who give promise of academic success, and the use of intelligence tests is widespread among them.   But, as has been noted in the previous chapter, the correlations between intelligence test scores and academic marks are low even with refined techniques, seldom being higher than .60, and averaging about .45.   Such a value is of little or no use for individual prediction.   Various devices to overcome this situation while still testing only intelligence are suggested.   Thus Johnston [42] and Thurstone [82] advocate a critical score method, and Rosenow [68] would have predictions reported for each intelligence level in terms of the probability of academic success.

That factors other than intelligence must be measured and incorporated into regression equations is felt increasingly necessary. Miss Rogers [67] points out that "obviously there are other factors" (than unreliability of criterion, in this case academic grades with a reliability of about .65) "that attenuate the correlation.   Temporary disturbances of health, emotional excitement and worry cause disagreement between test standing and college standing to some extent. The economic factor too is likely to enter in. . . .   Again, moral qualities such as the willingness to exert effort and to persist at a difficult task are perhaps the most significant factors."   And Charters [11] voices the conclusion of many investigators when he says of the correlations of .40 to .60 usually obtained, "This means merely that there is a slight tendency for bright students to make high grades in class, and it means nothing more.   In general, the brighter students make higher grades, but not often enough to give us much confidence in predicting more than that they *ought* to make higher grades.   That every student indicated as bright by the intelligence test will do so is never the case in any school. . . .   Deductions concerning scholastic success based upon intelligence rankings are wide open to criticism." He goes on to say, "The question regarding the existence of other possible factors which may influence school life is naturally raised. To this question common sense gives us some clues.   Everybody will tell you that character and personality are factors in success.   Executives will volunteer the information that industry—the ability to work hard and steadily—is a potent factor in success.   In some occupations social forcefulness and sociability are considered very important. The man of the street will undoubtedly tell you that the degree of interest in a vocation often spells the difference between success and failure. These are matters of common knowledge. University folk are inclined to overemphasize intellectual ability, while possibly the layman tends to underemphasize it." Charters' contention is that we must explore the clues provided in the field of personality, and he cites May's study [55] in predicting academic success, where the correlation between intelligence and grades was .60, that between industry (time spent in study) and grades was .32, and R, the coefficient of multiple correlation, between intelligence and industry together and grades rose to .82. He pleads for more careful use of results of tests, and for further work in rating scale techniques for personality factors. "We should have records not only of intelligence quotients and of educational marks, but of personality quotients as well. The student's record should contain not only his scholastic grades and his mental score, but his rating as well in certain fundamental traits of personality such as industry, ambition, friendliness, dependability, initiative, self-confidence, and resourcefulness. Only by these means can we hope approximately to predict his performance in succeeding grades or in his later adult life, and only from such data can we derive an index of his personal accomplishments." Though more recent writers put greater emphasis on the dynamic nature of personality than is suggested by Charters' use of the word "traits," they do not in the least disclaim the importance of such essentially non-intellectual aspects of personality as Charters and Miss Rogers indicate.

One factor which may reasonably be expected to play a part in determining college or normal school success is achievement up to the time of entrance. Crane [15] finds, as have others, that combining entrance examination scores with intelligence test scores improves prediction somewhat. The difficulty here is that intercorrelations between achievement tests and intelligence tests are usually undesirably high. Odell [65] has recently reported an extensive study in which complete high school records, intelligence test scores, and similar data on 2,000 cases were used to predict freshman marks in college. Multiple R's ranged between .60 and .70. Though these are encouraging, they are by no means all that could be desired, and because of the widely differing types of records submitted by high schools, the method calls for niceties of statistical handling not everywhere understood. Cannot personality factors be found which can be measured through test situations upon entrance and which with intelligence scores will yield predictions at least as high as these?

The study by May [55] mentioned by Charters gave the very high multiple R of .824. But the measure of industry which he used is a difficult one to secure, requiring the careful and conscientious keeping of diary records by students, and it cannot conveniently be administered at the outset of the term or before. Even though May's findings were corroborated generally, we would still not have a method of obtaining satisfactory prediction from tests given at or before entrance to the college or normal school.

Attempts to measure various factors of personality, emotional adjustment, and interests have been legion in the last few years. Several extensive bibliographies of these are available [51, 52, 56, 57, 66, 90, 91]. Because of the lack of standardized tests of sufficient reliability and validity in this field, not many studies have been made in connection with intelligence tests to obtain a prediction of academic success. Most of the investigations have been of an exploratory nature. It is apparent at once that the problem of validation in the field of personality and character tests presents peculiar difficulties, since many of the factors which it is desired to measure, especially in the realm of the emotions, may exist in a person without being known to his associates. This eliminates or at least throws into question validation by comparison of test scores with ratings of friends. Another difficulty is that certain factors must be measured without the subject knowing it, in order to circumvent defense reactions. Hence the indirect approach must often be used. Some of the attempts to devise measures for various aspects of personality will now be scanned.

Taking first the indirect approach, we find that questionnaires, in which many questions are asked and the real purpose is disguised or not easily apparent, have been used by Wells [93], by Lundberg [50], and by Shuttleworth [72, 73], to mention but three representative studies. Tests in which the purpose is disguised have been used by Brown [7] to measure "caution," Trow [85] to measure "confidence," Jones [43] to measure "certainty," "radicalism," and other supposed traits, Watson [89] to measure "fairmindedness," Knight [45] to determine the significance of "unwillingness to be tested."

The direct study of certain personality "traits" has been popular, proceeding along three lines. There have been, in the first place, ratings by associates, represented by such studies as that of Earle [17], Garrett [28], Hughes [39], Cogan, Conklin, and Hollingworth [12], Miner [59], Slaght [74], and Marsh and Perrin [53]. The wide use of such ratings has called forth numerous critical studies, of which the best known is that of Rugg [69], who has pointed out in an exhaustive study, based largely on his army experience, the conditions under which ratings may be relied upon.

In the second place, some use has been made of self-ratings, which have been found by Yoakum and Manson [94] to possess reasonable reliability, but the validity of which is made somewhat questionable by the tendency to overstatement found by Dorcus [16], Uhrbrock [87], Hollingworth [36], and Knight and Franzen [46].

In the third place, tests, either of the paper and pencil type or of conduct, have been used by Moss and Hunt [63] to measure "ability to get along with others"; by Gilliland and Burke [30] to measure "sociability" (part of this is in the form of a questionnaire); by Filter [18] to measure "self-assurance" and "speed of decision"; by Chambers [10], using the Pressey X O Tests, to measure emotional maturity and other emotional factors; by Furfey [27] to measure "developmental age"; by Burtt [8] in an attempt to measure interest; by Voelker [88] and by Hartshorne and May [33, 58] to measure conduct of various sorts. A diagnostic test which uses the paper and pencil technique to measure certain affective aspects of personality has been reported by Travis [84]. Chambers, using intelligence test scores, and Pressey X O Tests scored in a new way, obtains a multiple R of .56, which is somewhat higher than the usual correlation between intelligence and grades alone. Although the elaborate techniques of Hartshorne and May and their associates in the Character Education Inquiry constitute the classic work in the field of character and personality measurement thus far, their findings are not directly important for our problem of the value of measures of non-intellectual factors for the prediction of academic success in normal schools.

Measurement of the now familiar classification of personality as to degree of introversion or extraversion has received increasing attention from the experimentalists since it was first suggested by Jung. Among others who have written on this concept Freyd [23] lists Nicoll, Tansley, Hinkle, Kempf, White, Wells, Downey, McDougall, and Allport; and Schwegler [71], Marston [54], Newcomb [64], and others have studied it in relation to other factors. Following publication by Freyd [23] of a list of fifty-four traits thought to be associated with introversion, Heidbreder [34], at the University of Minnesota, arranged these in the form of a rating scale which she gave to two hundred students for both self-ratings and ratings by associates. She finds the scale traits consistent with each other and believes that taken together they give a picture of a fairly definite general attitude. Laird [49] has developed and used, both in the collegiate field at Colgate and elsewhere, and in the vocational world, the Personal Inventories C 2 and C 3 for measuring introversion and extraversion, which he finds of satisfactory reliability. In the first of these, self-ratings are used, and in the second, ratings by associates. Allport and Allport [1, 2] have recently brought out their scale for measuring "ascendance-submission," a concept seemingly related to the introversion-extraversion theory; this has been studied by Bender [4].

When we turn to the relationship between interests and abilities, we find that a good deal of experimental work has been done. Thorndike [80], in an early article, reported a high correlation (.89) between the interests of college students and their marks; and in a later article [81] refuted Bridges and Dollinger's 1920 data [5] which showed a correlation of only .25, revising this, by a different treatment of the data, to .46. He thinks that the true relationship between interest and ability "will surely rise above .70." This conclusion is questioned by Fryer [25], who by a different technique finds Thorndike's coefficient of .89 dropping to between .40 and .50, and hence in itself of little predictive value. Uhrbrock [86], reporting a study at the University of Wyoming, concludes that "from the point of view of those engaged in curriculum construction, and in employment management, the indication of interest probably should be given consideration." On the other hand, Hartman and Dashiell [32], in a somewhat limited experiment in which interest ranking of a test battery was correlated with performance ranking, found an average correlation of only .243, which would seem to lend weight to the position of Fryer, who says, in an article on predicting abilities from interests [26], "The facts are quite clear regarding the problem of the relation of interests and abilities. Interest expressions—vocational and educational ambitions —are of no significant value as criteria of abilities. This was found to be true both in the study of vocational and educational interests." The same writer, in another article [24], after reviewing the experimental evidence, concludes that interests have little value for vocational guidance. Kornhauser [47] reaches a similar conclusion regarding the interest type of questionnaire for predicting college success.

Yet efforts to build measures for the accurate determination of interests as an aid to both scholastic and vocational guidance go on apace. The Interests Analysis Blank, a paper and pencil technique developed by Freyd [21, 22] in which the subject indicates his like, indifference, or dislike for a large number of miscellaneous situations (274 in the Freyd scale), has been found by Hubbard [37, 38] to have reliabilities ranging from .49 to .62, which she considers to be highly satisfactory for an instrument attempting to measure such changeable factors as interests. Miner [60] has reported a similar technique yielding promising results. Cowdery [14] and Strong, Jr. [76, 77, 78], at Leland Stanford, have carried Freyd's technique into numerous vocational fields, revising and lengthening his blank to 420 items, and finding noticeable and significant differences in interests between various vocational and professional groups, so that Cowdery [14] remarks, "On the basis of expressed attitudes, obtained by means of a test situation in which is used the so-called Interests Report Blank, there is now available an objective professional classification of individuals which has proved its classificatory efficiency to be between 80 and 90 per cent, and the reliability of its scores to be from .77 to .90, according to the professional scale used and the educational level of the group considered." Thus, though the problem of the true relation of interests to abilities may be said to be still in doubt, at least one instrument that gives promise of being a satisfactory measure of interests is now in process of standardization. There seems to be no good reason why the Strong Interests Report Blank might not be standardized for academic success, and used with intelligence scores in multiple regression equations.

All of the various approaches mentioned thus far for measuring factors of personality leave out of account one very important consideration. Any psychiatrist will point out that to deal successfully with any problem behavior, one must first understand how the situation appears to the patient. It makes no difference how distorted or utterly fantastic his idea may be, reëducation and cure must be effected by starting from the point at which the patient thinks he is, rather than from where the psychiatrist may know that he really is. Applying this to our field of immediate interest, the accumulating experience of college personnel officers indicates that if a given college student, whose intelligence as measured by a good test is two S.D. above the mean for college students, has developed the belief that he is "dumb" and unable to do good scholastic work, the objective test record alone is likely to be rather misleading if used as a basis for prediction of success. Nor is the boy or girl of pleasing personality and considerable leadership ability, as judged by ratings of associates, likely to take a notable place as a social leader if he or she is convinced that every attempt at social prominence ends in failure and increased unpopularity. What is needed is a device that will measure these subjective feeling states, for evidence, clinical and otherwise, concerning their importance in everyday life is overwhelming. It has been suggested by Dr. Daniel Harrison Kulp II of Teachers College, in unpublished class discussion, that one's overt behavior is probably the result of a process of continual compromise and adjustment between at least four different "selves": a "naïve self," which is what one thinks of himself; an "objective self," which is what others think of him; a "mirrored self," which is what one thinks others think of him; and an "ideal self," which is what one wants others to think of him.

It is reasonable to suppose that were we able to measure adequately these various sorts of self-attitudes we should find each falling into a continuous distribution, probably conforming to the normal frequency surface. It is scarcely probable that a natural line of demarcation would exist dividing all persons into two groups, those who, let us say, feel "inferior" and those who do not. Rather, all experience in related fields of psychological measurement indicates that persons will think themselves more inferior or less so, and that any dividing line between persons who are on the whole hindered and those who are helped by their self-attitudes in this respect will ultimately have to be determined empirically. Presumably, it will be found that in a distribution of self-attitudes as to ability to succeed in what one undertakes, a line drawn near one end will set off that small group of persons (probably all too large, alas) who are rather seriously hampered in their efforts by constant thoughts of failure, from those who are not, in the main, so handicapped. Very probably, at the other end of the distribution a group might be set off whose overinflated ego actually constitutes a handicap, though they themselves are scarcely, or not at all, aware of it.

Of all the methods of study reported above, none gets at these subtle and various self-attitudes. The interests studies come the nearest to them, but information gained from them as to self-attitudes would be indirect and inferential; whereas it is the very essence of the importance of these attitudes that they be, as it were, photographed in their native habitat without any awareness of the photographer.

A technique which attempts to investigate certain of these self-attitudes is that first reported in 1922 by Knight and Franzen [46] and known as the Self-Ordinary-Ideal Rating Scale. This combines a modification of the Interests Report Blank with a device which makes possible a comparison of the "naïve self" with the "mirrored" and "ideal" selves. A number of other comparisons in this field of personal attitudes also become possible through this technique, as will be shown later. The subject is asked to rank each of a number of activities (thirty-four in the Knight-Franzen study), in order of (1) their interest to himself, (2) interest to the average person, and (3) interest to the ideal person. As used by Knight and Franzen, the scale served chiefly to give clear evidence of the well-nigh universal and now familiar tendency of individuals to rate themselves as nearer their own ideal than they conceive the average person to be. Watson and Chassell [92], in an attempt to study the possible significance for general emotional stability of such factors as large or small differences between ratings of self and ideal or self and group, included a short section of self-ordinary-ideal items in their experimental "Emotional History Record," revising the technique somewhat, so that instead of ranking the activities, the subject indicated degree of interest in each by means of a numerical scale.

The method seemed to offer promise and was incorporated into the extensive program of the Y. M. C. A. Character Growth Tests given over the country in 1926–1927 to boys between the ages of twelve and eighteen. It was used in a slightly different form and for another purpose in the Canadian Boys' Parliament in 1927. The extensive data from the Y. M. C. A. tests have been studied by Hall [31] and by Sweet [79], who find the technique highly reliable, various scores giving self-correlations ranging from .74 to .97. Sweet, carrying on investigations over the whole country, also finds reasonably satisfactory validity when scores are checked by ratings of leaders of the boys tested. He has standardized the test for boys of ages twelve to fourteen, and it may be said to have been amply demonstrated that the Self-Ordinary-Ideal Rating Scale, or the "Personal Attitudes Test," as Sweet terms it, is a useful instrument for getting at certain personality factors of boys of these ages.

Our problem concerns itself with the use of this general technique with undergraduate and graduate students in a teachers college. The specific form of test used is described on page 16. Samples of the test forms appear in the Appendix. The immediate question for which an answer will be sought is whether the use of this test technique, in combination with intelligence testing and certain other information readily obtainable from students upon entrance, will improve significantly our ability to predict academic success as measured by first semester marks.   Other problems to be considered include the reliability of the method and differences that may be found to exist between various academic groupings.   Some attempt will be made to interpret relationships found to be present between various scores, in so far as these may be considered to measure certain of the "self-attitudes" already mentioned.

CHAPTER III

DESCRIPTION OF DATA USED IN THE PRESENT STUDY

At the beginning of the fall semester at Teachers College in 1927 a general examination was given to all candidates for degrees. The examination was administered on two successive Saturday afternoons, three hours being used each week. As a result of this testing program, there were secured for each individual tested scores on each of the following tests: Thorndike Intelligence, Thorndike Reading, Wood-yard Reading, Thorndike Vocabulary,[1] as well as certain other tests which it was thought would yield valuable data but which have no connection with the present study, and finally, the Self-Ordinary-Ideal Scale here studied. Much of the material in the four tests first named was itself experimental in nature, and has itself formed the basis for intensive study by Krieger [48]; but enough is known about it from previous investigations of the Institute of Educational Research at Teachers College to justify the statement that the four tests taken together constitute a highly satisfactory measure of intelligence. Krieger [48 : 30] reports reliability coefficients, by the self-correlation method, to be, for the four tests, respectively, .885 ± .010, .891 ± .010, .772 ± .027, and .912 ± .008. Since no data were available when the present study was undertaken as to the optimum weighting of these four tests, the scores on each were T-scaled, and their mean was used as the measure of intelligence. Studying only graduate students, Krieger [48] found that the correlation between this average intelligence score and first semester marks was .459 ± .018, while the multiple correlation when the tests were given optimum weighting was only .473 ± .018. The use of the average T score as the measure of intelligence is thus justified, and in the pages that follow, whenever the "intelligence" of a student is mentioned, it is this mean T score of the four tests named above that is referred to.

Next, from the office of the registrar of the college, there were secured for each student (a) the department in which he was working, if a graduate student; (b) his age; and (c) the number of semester

---

[1] For a description of these four tests, see Krieger [48: 22].

hours of academic work completed during the term being studied, namely, the fall semester of 1927.

Finally, all of the class marks for this semester were T-scaled, according to the scheme detailed by Spence [75], and further described for these data by Krieger [48 : 24–28], and the mean T score for each person was computed. The reliability of this measure of academic success is found to be .653 when first and second semester marks are correlated.

The present study deals with the data from Part V of the General Examination battery, which was the Self-Ordinary-Ideal Rating Scale. The test, as there used, was of somewhat different form from that used by other experimenters. Like the usual Self-Ordinary-Ideal scale, it was made up of a series of unrelated items to which the subject was to respond by indicating in several ways his judgment as to degree of interest. Fifty-three such items were used in each of three forms, A, B, and C, of the test, but unlike other Self-Ordinary-Ideal scales, this one contained four columns for reactions instead of three. For each item the student was asked to indicate in the first, or S column, the degree of interest which he judged himself to possess; in the second, or O column, the degree of interest which he thought his friends, in general, judged him to possess; in the third, or G column, the degree of interest which he judged the average member of his professional group to possess; and in the fourth, or I column, the degree of interest which he judged he would possess if he were ideal. These judgments were all made in terms of an eleven-point numerical scale, in which o represented intense aversion, 5 indifference or neutrality, and 10 intense liking for or interest in. To distinguish the particular arrangement of the Self-Ordinary-Ideal Scale used here from others, it will be referred to henceforth as the SOGI Scale.

In the administration of the scale the three forms were rotated by chance, so that approximately equal numbers of each were used. As we have seen, each form consisted of 53 items, but only the first 28 differed in each form, the last 25 being the same for all. Thus a total of 109 different test items was available for study. These items had been used with groups which, because selected by chance, might be assumed to be of approximately equal ability and make-up. That this assumption is sound is shown by a statistical comparison of the three groups for certain factors. As Table I makes clear, no reliable differences were found between the means of the groups on the variables of academic marks, intelligence, efficiency (described on page 36),

TABLE I

COMPARISON, BY SOGI FORM TAKEN IN GENERAL EXAMINATION, OF STATISTICAL MEASURES AND RELIABILITY OF DIFFERENCES BETWEEN MEANS, FOR CERTAIN VARIABLES

VARIABLE	MEAN			S.D.			GROUPS COMPARED	DIFF. / S.D. DIFF.	CHANCES IN 100
	Form A	Form B	Form C	Form A	Form B	Form C			
	$N=457$	$N=467$	$N=440$						
Marks.......	51.00	50.67	51.09	6.30	6.30	6.56	AB	.80	79
							AC	.20	58
							BC	.98	84
Intelligence....	50.15	50.54	50.83	8.10	8.16	7.76	AB	.73	77
							AC	1.28	90
							BC	.55	71
Efficiency....	101.40	100.69	100.73	7.36	7.42	7.10	AB	1.46	93
							AC	1.37	91
							BC	.08	53
Age..........	32.43	32.12	31.89	7.44	7.70	7.20	AB	.62	73
							AC	1.11	86
							BC	.47	67
Hours........	14.32	14.21	14.32	3.02	3.16	2.98			

This table is read as follows: the mean marks score of the 457 students who took Form A of the SOGI Scale was 51.00, of those who took Form B, 50.67, of those who took Form C, 51.09. The standard deviations were, respectively, 6.30, 6.30, and 6.56. Between groups A and B, the difference in means divided by the standard deviation of the difference is .80, which means that the chances of a true difference are only 79 out of 100. The remainder of the table is read similarly.

or age. Although the variable of semester hours completed could not be treated statistically because its distributions were not normal, it will be noted that for two of the groups its means coincide, while the third differs by but .11. So far as these measures go, then, the three groups of students were equivalent. Any differences in scores found between different forms may therefore be considered due to inherent differences in the items themselves rather than in the groups to which the forms were given. A study of these items will be found in Chapter XI.

About 2,800 students were given the General Examination in October, 1927. T score averages of first semester marks were computed for only those students who completed eight or more semester hours during the term, regardless of the number for which they may originally have registered.   This fact reduced the number of cases available for this study to some 1,400.   The number was further reduced by the fact that some of these 1,400 students were found not to have filled out the SOGI Scale completely.   If a person had made only occasional omissions, not exceeding 10 per cent of the four times 53, or 212 expected responses, his paper was retained.   Papers with more than 10 per cent of the responses missing were ruled out.   The total number of cases finally retained for study was 1,364, of which 245 were papers of men students and 1,119 were papers of women students.

There were 457 Form A papers, 467 Form B, and 440 Form C. Papers filled out by undergraduate students, candidates for the B.S. degree, numbered 565; by graduate students, candidates for the M.A. or Ph.D. degree, 799.   Table II gives the distributions by sex, academic status, and form.

TABLE II

DIVISION OF DATA BY FORMS

	FORM A		FORM B		FORM C		TOTAL
	Under-graduates	Graduates	Under-graduates	Graduates	Under-graduates	Graduates	
Men.........	8	76	14	83	13	51	245
Women......	181	192	171	199	178	198	1,119
Total......	189	268	185	282	191	249	1,364

CHAPTER IV

METHODS OF SCORING THE SOGI SCALE

The first problem was the development of a satisfactory scoring scheme. Numerous possibilities presented themselves, yielding a considerable number of variables. Accordingly, it was decided to study a sampling of the papers intensively, scoring these in a number of different ways, in order to find the plan which would give the best predictive power to the scale. To eliminate differences that might be due to differences between forms, the sampling was chosen exclusively from one form, Form A, and a sampling of 102 papers was secured by taking alternately every fourth and every fifth paper from the data as arranged alphabetically. That the sample of 102 Form A papers is a true and representative sample of the 457 Form A papers in the entire body of data is shown by a statistical comparison of the means and S.D.'s of the two groups. For the five variables, Marks, Intelligence, Efficiency, Hours Completed, and Age, there are no significant differences between the sample and the larger group. Moreover, of the twelve different scores investigated for all the Form A papers, not one shows a significant difference in mean between the sample and the larger group. These facts are brought out by Table III. We may accordingly conclude that the sample is a good one, adequately representing the entire body of Form A data.

It will be seen that there are two possibilities in the use of the SOGI Scale. One is as a measure of interests. Here the S or Subjective column would be the only one used, and it would be treated much as Cowdery and Strong, Jr., have done with Freyd's scale. That is, items differential as between various professional or academic groups would be sought, and by means of numerous scoring keys the field with which a given student was most nearly in harmony would be found. Since Freyd's scale consists of some 274 items, and Strong's revision of 420, as against but 53 for the SOGI Scale, it will be seen that for this purpose our SOGI data are inferior. If the length of the scale were increased to make it comparable with even the Freyd scale, while retaining the four column form for S, O, G, and I responses, the

TABLE III

RELIABILITIES OF DIFFERENCES BETWEEN SCORES ON ALL FORM A PAPERS AND
FORM A SAMPLE

SCORE	ALL FORM A (N = 457)		FORM A SAMPLE (N = 102)		DIFF. S. D. DIFF.	CHANCES IN 100
	Mean	S. D.	Mean	S. D.		
Marks.........	51.00	6.30	50.16	5.98	1.27	89
Intelligence.....	50.16	8.10	49.88	7.84	.32	62
Efficiency......	101.42	7.34	100.82	6.88	.79	79
Hours..........	14.32	3.02	13.88	3.10	1.30	90
Age............	32.43	7.46	32.65	7.70	.26	60
SO *..........	41.24	21.54	42.26	22.16	.42	65
SG...........	61.46	27.70	63.72	29.91	.70	76
SI............	63.72	24.31	64.22	25.87	.18	57
OG...........	59.00	26.38	61.27	27.30	.76	77
OI............	77.06	27.80	78.72	26.36	.57	72
GI............	81.20	31.91	83.24	28.49	.64	74
Ss............	65.87	14.30	64.07	15.20	1.10	86
Ii............	56.42	14.50	56.12	18.20	.16	56
Gs............	65.74	18.65	64.85	22.00	.38	65
GI − SI.......	18.26	31.50	19.51	32.28	.36	64
SG − OG......	3.14	16.42	2.16	18.52	.49	69
OI − SI.......	13.87	17.00	14.22	16.25	.19	58

Table III is read similarly to Table I.

* For explanation of the meaning of the scores here referred to, see pages 21–25.

time required for the use of the SOGI Scale would be between two and a half and three hours. Such a change is inadvisable, as it would make the taking too monotonous. That even a short series of items on which the subject indicates his interest might be found to be of some value for prediction may be inferred from a recent study by Morris [61], in which a series of 46 items on which the subject indicates degrees of like or dislike is used as part of a test battery for predicting teaching success. She reports its scores forming about 30 per cent of a composite "Trait Index" score which correlates .342 with academic averages for two years in a teacher-training institution, and .512 with success in practice teaching. In view of these considerations, this study will take no account of the SOGI Scale as an interests measure.

The other possibility in the SOGI Scale is found in its use as a measure of certain personality or emotional factors presumably having to do with the subject's conception of himself and his relations with other people. Here the concern is with the differences found between the person's judgments of himself, as shown by the S column, and his responses in other columns. These may be considered in some detail. It is to be emphasized in this discussion that explanations of probable meanings of scores are purely deductive, resting at this point on no objective validation. To reënforce this word of caution, each score will be referred to hereafter by the letters of the columns determining it.

A. "INDIVIDUAL SCORES"

1. *SO Differences*

In the first place, there is the difference between the subject's judgments of himself and his judgments as to what other people think of him. This is shown by the differences between his S responses and his O responses. It seems reasonable to suppose that a person who shows a large aggregate of differences here, differs in some way from the person who shows few or no differences—as the student who wrote in the O column, "Same as the S column, I don't consider myself a misunderstood woman." Two further differences may be noted here: on the one hand, the person who rates himself nearer his own ideal than he thinks others would rate him; and on the other hand, the person who judges that others think him nearer what he conceives as ideal than he considers himself to be. These will be discussed later (see OI — SI Scores).

2. *SG Differences*

Next, there is the difference between the subject's idea of himself and his idea of the average person. Some confusion probably is found here because although the students were directed to consider the average person in their own professional group, e. g., school administrators, elementary school teachers, etc., it seems probable from comments made by some students later that many simply thought of the average person of their acquaintance or the average educator. Whether this confusion introduces an error or not is open to question. It is at least possible that any given person will tend to show about the same differences between his own ratings and his ratings of the average person whether average ratings of his general acquaintances, his professional group, or the general educational field be taken. In other words, our scale may be measuring fairly consistent general tendencies rather than specific accuracies of judgment. In this score there are again two possibilities. Some persons will rate the group as distinctly lower, i. e., further from their own ideal than themselves, and others will rate themselves lower than the group. (See GI — SI Scores.) It is reasonable to suppose that real differences in personality make-up are represented by these opposing reactions and by degrees of differences which the person thinks exist between himself and his group.

3. *SI Differences*

In the third place, we have differences between the subject's idea of himself and his conception of what he would be were he ideal. To what extent such differences represent emotional conflict, and to what extent simply recognized differences to which the subject is well adjusted, is not known. Presumably, unless real conflict exists, there will be little or no relationship between SI difference and academic success. Where such conflict does exist, it may be supposed to constitute, to some extent, a handicap to most effective scholastic endeavor.

4. *OG Differences*

Differences found between other columns, not involving the S ratings, may also be significant. These give three more scores, of which the first is OG differences. What is probably represented here is harder to see. It would seem to be the difference between what the subject thinks other people judge him to be and what he judges others to be. The person with small difference here may perhaps be thought of as the one who feels that he is generally considered about average, fitting in well with the group, conforming to what is expected or thought usual; while the person with large differences is he who thinks he is looked upon as "peculiar." In comparing myself with the group it is the opinion of me which I judge others to hold rather than my own opinion of myself which determines how much "at home" I feel in the group; hence this score may prove to be more valuable than at first appears.

5. *OI Differences*

Next, differences between the O and I columns may be noted. These would seem to represent the gap between what a person believes others think about him and what he believes is ideal for himself; that is, how far he believes his reputation to differ from what would be his own ideal.

6. *GI Differences*

There is, lastly in this set of scores, the difference between the G and I columns, that is, the person's judgment as to how far the group differs from what he conceives to be ideal for himself.   A large score would indicate harsh judgment of the group, i. e., that the individual rates the group far from ideal.   This gives us six scores, based on differences between various columns of individual papers.

In addition to these six scores derived by comparison of the respective columns of an individual's responses, it is also possible to derive several scores based on a comparison of individual with group responses.

B.   "Group-Individual Scores"

1.   *Ss Differences*

If for the whole group we tabulate the responses to each item for the S column, we get a picture of the actual interests of the group as the individuals themselves judge them.   The interests of any person may be compared with these group interests and a "peculiarity of interest" measure, here called the Ss Score, secured.   A person with a large Ss score may be thought to be one whose likes and dislikes differ considerably from those of the average person.

2.   *Ii Differences*

In the same way that the composite or group S interests were obtained, we may get a picture of the group ideals from the I column. By comparing these group ideals with individual ideals a "peculiarity of ideal" score may be gained, which we call the Ii Score.   A large Ii score is taken as indicative of ideals notably different from those of most people.

3.   *Gs Differences*

In the G column of the scale the subjects were asked to give their estimate of the interest of the average person in each of the test items. Through tabulation of the S column we are now in a position to know what this interest actually is.   We may therefore compare these actual group interests with the individual G column, securing a score that indicates the accuracy of judgment or "insight" of each person. This score we may call the Gs Score.   A large Gs score indicates poor "insight" in this particular task, i. e., that the individual has greatly misjudged the actual interests of the group.

C.   "Three-Column Scores"

Several scores were investigated which necessitate a comparison of relationships between three columns.   Of these, the first two may be considered as possible measures of the degree of inferiority feeling, or the reverse, possessed by an individual.

1. *GI minus SI Score*

It is noticeable that most people rate the G column as further from the I column than they do the S column. That is, most persons tend to rate themselves as nearer to their own ideal than they believe the average person to be. This fact has been thoroughly established by Knight and Franzen [46] and others. It is borne out by our study. The difference between a person's GI and SI scores may be considered a measure of "superiority" or "inferiority." If it is positive, it indicates that the SI differences were less than the GI; that is, that the person judges himself nearer the ideal than he judges the group to be; or, in general, that he appears to think himself "superior." If it is negative, it indicates that the GI differences were less than the SI; that is, that the individual judges the group as nearer his ideal than he judges himself to be; or, in general, that he seems to think himself "inferior." This score will be called the GI − SI Score.

2. *SGI Score*

In the six "Individual scores" (A, above) no account of direction of difference is taken. Hence no account of direction of original differences is taken in deriving the GI − SI score just described. It is possible, however, to score the papers by comparing the S, G, and I columns simultaneously, counting SG differences as positive or negative according as the S or the G response is nearer to the I. This gives, then, a second total score which may be thought to measure the individual's superiority or inferiority self-attitude. It is called the SGI Score. Because of the similarity in their derivation, these two methods of scoring for inferiority are of necessity highly correlated, the coefficient being .974 ± .004. It is presumable that they measure about the same factors, and because the GI − SI is far more simple to secure, we shall expect to discard the SGI scores unless they prove to be, for some reason, of considerably more value for predictive purposes than the GI − SI scores are.

3. *OI minus SI Score*

By comparing the OI and SI scores we may get a measure of the person's ideas concerning his reputation. Thus, if his SI score is greater than his OI, he rates himself further from his ideal than he thinks others consider him. If, on the other hand, the OI is greater than the SI, he judges himself more nearly ideal than he believes he is considered. With the subtraction carried out as indicated, OI − SI, a positive score means that the person judges himself more easily than he thinks others judge him; a negative score, that he judges himself more harshly than he thinks others judge him. This may perhaps be taken to mean that a positive score indicates one who feels his reputation poorer than his character warrants; and a negative score, one who feels his reputation better than his character warrants, if we may amend the familiar saying to read, "Reputation is what others think you are; character is what you think you are." The tendency of people to judge themselves too easily is found again here.

4. *SG minus OG Score*

Of the fifteen possible comparisons involving two of the six "Individual scores," one more seemed to offer theoretical possibilities. This was the comparison of SG and OG. Here, if OG be subtracted from SG, a negative result would be taken to mean that the individual rates himself judged by others as being more different from the average than he himself thinks he is; while a positive result would mean that he rates himself more different than he believes others think him.

D. "Extremes Score"

Finally, it was thought that the tendency to extreme as against moderate judgments might be significant. Perhaps the person whose paper is liberally sprinkled with 9's and 10's or with 0's and 1's is the enthusiastic individual who becomes excited easily and cools off rapidly, the person with "hair-trigger" emotional responses. This score, which is comparable to Morris' score of "emotional intensity" [62], consists simply of the total number of 9, 10, 0, and 1 responses in all four columns, and is called here the "Extremes Score."

This gives us, in all, for study, fourteen scores, two of which are practically identical.

Coming now to the actual scoring several problems arise. First, in securing the six "Individual scores," SO, SG, SI, OG, OI, and GI, shall we consider total amount of difference, or only the number of items on which difference exists? For example, in scoring SO, if a person answers a given item 6 for S and 8 for O, shall we count two points toward his score, representing the actual difference, or only one point, representing the fact that on this item difference exists? Sweet [79], in his investigation of the Self-Ordinary-Ideal technique with boys, found the second method sufficient. Obviously it is easier to score. To answer the question for our data, we need to determine (*a*) the reliabilities of both types of scores, and (*b*) their respective correlations with the chief criterion of our study, namely, marks. We shall call the first type of score "Total Deviation Scores," and the second, "Number-of-Question Deviation Scores."

Again, in the Group-Individual scoring at least two possibilities appear. The problem is to find which responses represent the group, and which may be taken as indicating peculiarity. After tabulating the responses in the S and I columns, item by item, we may (*a*) take the mean, to the nearest integer, as best representing the group attitude, and count deviations from this as to amount; or (*b*) we may calculate for each item the percentage of persons giving each response, and set an arbitrary limit between "peculiar" and "normal" percentages, getting a person's score by counting the number of "peculiar" responses. In the first method, which corresponds to the "Total Deviation" method of deriving the Individual scores, if the mean S response for a certain item were 6.7, we should call this 7, and give a person who responded 4 an Ss score of 3 for this item. In the second method, which corresponds to the "Number-of-Question Deviation" Individual scores, if the response 4 were given by less than the percentage of students arbitrarily agreed upon, this individual would be given an Ss score of 1 for this item. Since our scale contained eleven divisions, 0 through 10, it was decided to set 9 per cent as the point of division; for, were the judgments evenly divided over the scale, each would have about 9 per cent of the total, and accordingly any response getting less than this normal quota would be a disfavored, or "peculiar" response. A scoring key was made up on this basis. Sweet, in the study referred to above, found this percentage method the best of several which he compared for getting the "Group-Individual scores." As in the Individual scoring methods, we shall determine which plan is superior for our purpose by the respective correlations with the criterion, marks, and with other secondary criteria.

In obtaining the Group-Individual scores by the method of deviations from the mean group responses, it is of practical interest to inquire whether the tabulations of responses must be made for all of the data or whether a sufficiently accurate group norm is obtained from a sample. Obviously the saving in time will be considerable if the latter should prove true. To answer this question, the 84 men's papers of Form A were scored by the key made up from tabulation of the 102 Form A papers of the sample, all but 14 of which were women's papers. They were then rescored by a key made up by a tabulation of the responses on all the data, i. e., on all the Form A men's papers. The means of the three scores, Ss, Ii, and Gs, as scored by the two methods agreed very closely, none of the differences being statistically significant. The pairs of scores correlated highly, moreover, the coefficients in order being .94, .94, and .93. It may be concluded that in the use of the SOGI Scale, a sample of about 100 cases gives adequate group norms for scoring Ss, Ii, and Gs by the use of the mean group response. If the Group-Individual scores are obtained by counting the number of the individual's "peculiar" responses, presumably the papers of the whole group tested should be used.

CHAPTER V

RELIABILITY OF SOGI SCORES

We are now ready to inquire into the reliability of the scores obtained from the SOGI Scale. How consistently does each measure whatever it does measure? Several methods may be followed in reaching an answer to this question. The two principal ones are the retest and the split-half techniques, both of which were used in this study. They will be reported separately.

A. THE RETEST

If the same test be given twice to the same group of persons, and the pairs of scores correlated, we have a fairly clear-cut answer to the question of the test's reliability. But people tend to be influenced to some extent the second time by their first responses, and some are so influenced more than are others. The giving of a second form for the retest helps to obviate this difficulty, and was resorted to here.

From the class rolls of two classes in educational psychology, the names of all those students who had taken the SOGI Scale in October and who had completed eight or more semester hours during the fall semester, were selected. One of these classes was a large one composed of graduates studying the psychology of character. The other was an undergraduate group, much smaller in number, in an elementary course in educational psychology. Through an error in the list which was consulted, it developed that all but two of these undergraduates who were retested had taken the test not in October, but in February. There were 19 of these. Though their original papers were not included in the data of this study, they were secured and used for the reliability study. It was believed that their inclusion would not materially alter the results, since the original tests had been taken under comparable conditions, and since in both instances considerable time had elapsed between the test and the retest. We had, then, 73 retests from persons who had been tested first in October, and 19 retests from persons tested first in February, a total of 92 papers. Since it was impossible to require the students selected to take the test again, their coöperation was enlisted, and of 101 papers given out, all but 9 were returned. The following statement was made at the time of giving out the retests:

> Copies of an attitudes test are being passed to a sampling of the students in this class. It is thought that students in this class will be glad to coöperate in the study of this technique for getting at personality factors. Since the test is still experimental, it is hoped that those who receive it will be careful to see that every copy is returned.
>
> Will those who receive the test please fill it out at some convenient time within a week, and return it to this class or to the psychology office? Even though you have taken the test before, please do it carefully and frankly. It is understood that the scores are not to be used in any personal way, but for statistical study only.

The retests were distributed to the graduate class on May 2, 1928, and to the undergraduate class on the following day.

It will be noted that if we assume that this test does give a reliable measure of the factors of personal adjustment suggested in the preceding chapter, we should expect the coefficients to be somewhat low, since (*a*) each person took a different form on the retest than on the original test, and we have no data as yet to show that the three forms are equivalent; and (*b*) we may be measuring in the retest not only reliability but change as well. This change might be presumed to be considerable over a winter spent in a stimulating city and college atmosphere. The correlations obtained in this part of our investigation must be thought of then as influenced by both of these factors. These coefficients are given in Table IV, Column 1, and for the six Individual scores range between .51 and .62, averaging .56. The probable errors are in no case greater than .05.

The influence of the changed forms may be removed if we confine our attention to the last twenty-five items, which were the same for all forms. Computing the reliability coefficients for this last half alone, and applying the Spearman-Brown Prophecy Formula to obtain the approximate coefficients to be expected from the whole test of 53 items, gives us somewhat higher coefficients, ranging, for the six Individual scores, from .64 to .76, and averaging .69. (Table IV, Column 2.) That these coefficients are still markedly lower than the split-half reliabilities next to be considered may probably be ascribed mainly to the factor of change mentioned above; for it seems scarcely likely that practice effect, i. e., memory of responses made the first time, would exercise an appreciable influence over so long a period of time.

B. The Split Test

1. *Individual Scores*

a. First-half: last-half Reliability. Since the papers were originally scored so as to give separate scores on the first 28 questions and on the last 25 questions, a reliability study was made by correlating the scores on these two parts of the scale, and applying the Prophecy Formula. Here we find, Table IV, Column 3, that for the six Individual scores the average reliability is .82, which is considerably higher than the retest average of .56, and lends support to the assumption that the retest scores measure actual changes in the factors studied.

b. Odd-Even Reliability. Further evidence as to the reliability of the six Individual scores is obtained from correlations between the odd and even items scored separately. After the Prophecy Formula has been applied, we have even higher correlations than were found for the first-half: last-half, with an average of .895. These coefficients are obtained from the "Total Deviation" scores. We may next inquire as to the reliability of the more rapidly scored "Number-of-Question Deviation" scores. Using the odd-even method and the Prophecy Formula as above, reliabilities are obtained, Table IV, Column 5, which average .803 as compared with the average of .895 for these same scores obtained by the "Total Deviation" method. To raise the reliabilities of the "Number-of-Question Deviation" scores from .80 to .90 would require lengthening the test to 119 items. This is clearly impractical. Further, in every case the reliability of the "Number-of-Question Deviation" score is inferior to that of the "Total Deviation" score. Unless it should develop that the former method gives superior correlations with marks and other criteria, the "Number-of-Question Deviation" method will not be used.

It may be noted in passing, however, that on the whole the reliabilities of the six Individual scores, even when the scores are secured by the more rapid "Number-of-Question Deviation" method, compare favorably with many tests in use to-day.

2. *Group-Individual Scores*

The reliability of the Ss, Ii, and Gs scores, which were found for the 102 Form A papers by both of the methods of scoring described in Chapter IV, was studied by the odd-even method. These scores are found to be somewhat less reliable than the six Individual scores, averaging .79 for the "Deviation from Mean" method and .78 for the "Number of Less than 9 per cent Responses" method. The differences in reliability between the two methods are insignificant, and their direction does not consistently favor either. The "Deviation from Mean" method, however, is far easier to derive and score. It will, therefore, be used unless it turns out that the other method gives superior correlations with the criteria.

3. *Remaining Scores*

In the same manner, by the odd-even method, the reliabilities of the remaining five scores were determined. Of these five, the SGI and Extremes scores each showed reliabilities of .90. The GI − SI and SG − OG gave coefficients of .85, and the OI − SI showed a reliability of .66.

C. Internal Evidence of Reliability

Can we be sure that these relatively high coefficients prove the SOGI scores to be reliable to this extent? It is possible that persons taking the test develop a pattern response which tends to operate rather consistently throughout the whole test. If this be true, our correlations might be high, especially when obtained through the odd-even technique; yet obviously the test would be of little value. If pattern responses prevail to any considerable extent, the test is measuring only the extent to which individuals do make such pattern responses. In such an event, our reliability coefficients simply show that the patterns are relatively consistent. In an attempt to solve this difficulty, two questions may be considered.

1. Is there evidence that persons tend to give the same response in all four columns? If any person did this consistently throughout the test, it is clear that his six Individual scores would be uniformly zero. We have no such papers in our data. Using the sampling of 102 Form A papers, a count was made of the number of times that each individual marked all four columns the same on an item. The following distribution resulted:

No. of Items Having 4 Columns Alike	Items 1–28	Items 29–53	Whole Test
32–35	—	—	0
28–31	—	—	1
24–27	0	0	1
20–23	0	0	0
16–19	0	1	4
12–15	4	1	6
8–11	2	6	14
4–7	25	26	32
0–3	71	68	44
	102	102	102

It appears that few persons mark very many items the same way in all four columns. Considering the whole test, only about 25 per cent used more than 15 per cent of their chances to rate items the same across all four columns; i. e., only 26 of the 102 papers showed more than 7 items rated alike all the way across. Conversely, we have 75 per cent of persons using less than 15 per cent of their chances to rate columns alike. Moreover, there is, of course, no way of being sure that when a person rates a given item the same in all four columns he is doing so because he has built up a habit pattern or through carelessness; he may sincerely believe that the four columns ought to be rated alike on that item. Again, the fact that the last half of the test shows only a very slight tendency to have more items answered alike for all columns gives additional weight to the conclusion that no serious tendency to pattern responses of this sort can be found.

2. Is there evidence that persons tend to build up a particular pattern response which they use repeatedly? This would mean the use of a given combination, such as 7 6 4 8, rather consistently for a number of items. Any pronounced tendency to do this would influence our results, as it would indicate that the rater was probably careless in his work, and not giving each item serious consideration. Such recurring individual patterns would be expected to show up most clearly in the last half of the test, if at all. Accordingly, a count was made of the total number of times that items in the last half of the test were answered by the use of any given pattern. The result is:

Number of Items Answered by Same Pattern	Frequency
10	1
9	1
8	0
7	1
6	3
5	12
4	16
3	26
2	39
0	3
	102

From this it appears that the majority of persons, even in the last part of the test, where patterns would be expected to show up if at all, used the same pattern response to answer not more than 3 of the 25 items. About 83 per cent used not more than 16 per cent of their chances to respond by patterns. No papers were found in which a pattern was apparently used indiscriminately throughout. In most instances, persons tend to develop several patterns, each of which may be used twice or perhaps three times. Often a person adopts a type pattern, changing the numbers used, but keeping the same relative position for several items, though rarely consecutively, thus: 9 10 8 10, 7 8 6 8. Only one paper was found in which any given pattern was used consecutively more than four times. This all seems adequate evidence of the fact that the students who took the test gave it reasonably careful attention, and we may safely assume that their responses represent their best rapid judgment—rapid because the test was administered at the close of a three-hour testing period, when people were becoming anxious to leave, but none the less valuable on that account. Indeed, rapid judgments, relatively unrationalized, are precisely what we wish in a scale of this type.

D. Conclusions as to Reliability

The almost unanimous testimony of persons who take the SOGI Scale is that it must be very unreliable. All the evidence, on the contrary, indicates that its various scores compare favorably in reliability with the general run of intelligence and achievement tests now in use. The average reliability of all the "Total Deviation" scores is .85, the range being .66 to .93; that of the "Number-of-Question Deviation" scores is .73, with a range of .65 to .91. There is, as has been shown, internal evidence of the test's consistency. The lower coefficients, averaging .56, obtained by retesting after several months, may indicate that we are measuring changes in self-group and other attitudes.

That the correlations from the retest, using (in part) different test items, are as high as they are, is striking evidence that the SOGI Scale measures reliably some characteristics of individuals. Further investigations along this line have been carried on by Dr. Raymond Franzen, but have not as yet been published. In a letter to the writer he states, speaking of the tendency to judge the group farther from the ideal than the self is, "that there are individual differences in the qualities indicated, and that individual differences in these qualities are reliable in the sense that distinctions between individuals occur in a like manner with different sets of materials."

It is true that the reliabilities shown are below the coefficient of .94 suggested by Kelley [44] as requisite for tests designed for use in individual diagnosis. This greater reliability might be secured by lengthening the test. Taking the average "Total Deviation" reliability of .85, and working the Prophecy Formula backwards, we find that to get the desired average coefficient of .94 our scale would have to be 2.76 times its present length.   This would give us 146 items.   Such a test would be monotonously long to take, and its length would doubt- less tend to increase pattern responses, carelessness, and other unde- sirable features.   It may be pointed out, moreover, that few tests in common use for individual guidance and diagnosis measure up to the reliability standard which Kelley urges.   If the more reliable of our SOGI scores prove of value in the prediction of academic success, we may safely conclude that these measures are of sufficient reliability for practical purposes.

Finally, although the "Total Deviation" scores are somewhat more reliable than those secured by the easier and more rapid "Number-of- Question Deviation" method, the differences are not great.   The decision as to which method should be adopted in further use of the SOGI Scale may, therefore, be left until we have compared the corre- lations which the two methods give with marks and other criteria.

TABLE IV: RELIABILITY COEFFICIENTS OF SOGI SCALE SCORES

SCORE	TOTAL DEVIATION SCORES				NUMBER-OF-QUESTION DEVIATION SCORES
	RETEST (N = 92)		SPLIT TEST (N = 102)		SPLIT TEST (N = 102)
	With Different Form	With Same Items	First-half: Last-half	Odd-Even	Odd-Even
Column No.	1	2	3	4	5
SO............	.57 ± .048	.66 ± .040	.86 ± .018	.93 ± .009	.91 ± .011
SG............	.58 ± .048	.76 ± .030	.83 ± .021	.92 ± .010	.87 ± .016
SI............	.51 ± .052	.64 ± .042	.86 ± .018	.88 ± .015	.84 ± .020
OG............	.59 ± .046	.71 ± .035	.77 ± .027	.90 ± .013	.67 ± .037
OI............	.51 ± .052	.68 ± .038	.84 ± .020	.86 ± .018	.80 ± .024
GI............	.62 ± .044	.70 ± .036	.77 ± .027	.88 ± .015	.73 ± .031
Ss............				.77 ± .027	.76 ± .028
Ii............				.79 ± .025	.71 ± .033
Gs............				.80 ± .024	.86 ± .018
SGI..........				.90 ± .013	.87 ± .016
Extremes......				.90 ± .013	
GI − SI.......				.85 ± .019	.84 ± .020
SG − OG.....				.85 ± .019	.69 ± .035
OI − SI.......				.66 ± .038	.65 ± .039
Average.....	.563	.692	.822	.849	.729

CHAPTER VI

VALIDITY OF SOGI SCORES FOR PREDICTION
OF ACADEMIC SUCCESS

"The validity of any measuring instrument depends on the fidelity with which it measures whatever it purports to measure." [29 : 266] But often a test may be used successfully even though its objective validity be not known. This is true, for example, of intelligence tests. Although there is not even general agreement as to the precise meaning of the term intelligence, thousands of children are given "intelligence" tests yearly. Nor is this fact to be interpreted as a disparagement of the testing, for although we cannot be sure that by the tests we have measured the actual intelligence of the children, we do know beyond doubt that the tests measure something which is in a definite way related to the quality of school work of which the children will be capable. And such knowledge has distinct value. To quibble over the objective validity of intelligence tests, meanwhile neglecting to use them, would be as foolish as refusing to use an electric meter until there was complete knowledge as to the precise nature of electricity. For practical uses we know beyond doubt that intelligence tests are valid for purposes of enabling us to know more accurately how to place and educate a given individual. And we know this simply because, given adequate reliability, we get consistently significant correlations between "intelligence" scores and various measures of school success. In just this same way we shall conclude that the SOGI Scale is or is not valid. We have found it to measure reliably some quality or qualities of individuals. The precise names of these qualities may be safely left for future investigation to determine, and we shall here avoid any certain conclusions as to names, venturing only a few guesses. But the technique will be valid for our purpose if it can be shown that it improves significantly our ability to foretell the quality of academic work which a given individual will do in a teacher-training institution.

There is another phase of the problem of validity which may be mentioned here, although it bears essentially upon the problem of ascertaining the objective or true validity rather than upon the pragmatic or working validity just mentioned. When we attempt to measure such factors as emotional adjustment, feelings of inferiority, and the like, it is impossible to validate by getting the judgments of friends of our subjects as to whether or not the subjects really do possess the feelings in question. Many times the possessor of such attitudes successfully hides them from his friends. The important fact is that he possesses them, whether or not others know it, and whether or not there is any justification for such feelings. Nor are such persons likely to give very trustworthy replies if asked themselves directly as to their feelings. It would probably be possible, through a carefully worked out series of intensive case studies, to throw some light on what personality characteristics, if any, the SOGI Scale scores correspond to. This has not been undertaken in the present study, however, which relies simply on the working validity which the Scale may be found to have for the prognostic purpose at hand.

With this purpose in mind, we are now ready to set up our criteria. The chief criterion is, of course, academic marks. The method of securing the average T-scaled mark for each person has already been mentioned. SOGI Scores correlating highly with marks may be scores which will aid our prediction of these marks. Whether they will be or not depends, however, on the correlations of such scores with intelligence, since it is also to be one of the variables in our final regression equation. Therefore, the intelligence scores may be regarded as a second criterion. The third criterion may be called "efficiency," and we may well note at this point its meaning.

When both academic marks and intelligence test scores are expressed in common units such as S.D. units or the McCall T scores, the net influence of all the factors other than intelligence (as measured by the intelligence test used) upon the determination of any student's marks may be expressed as the difference between his mark T score and his intelligence T score. That is to say, from a person's intelligence score and his efficiency score, a perfect prediction of marks may be made. The efficiency score embraces the influence of all the various personality and adjustment factors mentioned previously, some of which probably are in themselves related in varying degrees to intelligence. For convenience, we may express this efficiency score as a number greater or less than 100, understanding a score of 100 to stand for a case in which intelligence and marks scores are equal. Then a person whose marks score is less than his intelligence score will have an efficiency score less than 100, and he whose marks score is greater than his intelligence score will be given an efficiency score greater than 100. The formula for deriving the efficiency score is:

$$\text{Marks} - \text{intelligence} + 100 = \text{efficiency.}$$

It is to be noted that where the efficiency score is 100, the implication is not necessarily that no other factors than intelligence condition the marks score, but rather that in this instance the nonintellectual factors cancel each other, some working positively and others negatively, their net effect being zero. A similar condition exists for each other efficiency score, with some factors working to raise marks and others to lower them, only here the net result is something other than zero. On the whole, academic success is to be thought of as the result of an immensely complicated interplay of forces, some quite closely related, some totally unrelated, some antagonistic to each other. By analogy, we may think of the degree of academic success achieved by any individual as the resultant of all these forces, so that, were adequate measures of all the forces available, it might be determined in similar fashion to the familiar "composition of forces" problem in physics. We shall, therefore, expect to find all degrees of both positive and negative correlation between various factors which may be measured as the analysis of academic success progresses, and all degrees of relationship with the criteria of marks, intelligence, and efficiency.

We are now in a position to examine and compare the correlations with the three criteria obtained for each score by each of the two scoring methods, "Total Deviation" and "Number-of-Question Deviation." These are shown in Table V. In each cell where two coefficients appear, the upper is the "Total Deviation" coefficient, and the lower is the "Number-of-Question Deviation" coefficient. For clearness, probable errors are not given in this table, but their amount is, in general, about .06. Hence, no coefficients smaller than about .25 can be regarded as surely indicative of relationship.

Examination of the table reveals the fact that the "Total Deviation" scores in the main give higher correlations with the criteria than do the "Number-of-Question Deviation" scores. Of coefficients of .20 or more, and thus almost certainly indicative of true relationship greater than zero, there are eight among the "Total Deviation" scores and but three among the "Number-of-Question Deviation" scores. These facts, together with the tendency for the "Total

TABLE V

COEFFICIENTS OF CORRELATION OF SOGI SCALE SCORES WITH CRITERIA

SCORES	CRITERIA		
	Marks	Intelligence	Efficiency
SO..........................	− .177	− .245	.145
	− .122	− .144	.071
SG..........................	.026	− .124	.184
	− .012	− .057	.076
SI...........................	− .137	− .006	− .096
	− .031	.147	− .171
OG..........................	.019	− .100	.149
	.015	.014	.017
OI...........................	− .127	− .043	− .042
	− .053	.087	− .122
GI...........................	.059	− .078	.169
	.109	.118	− .005
Ss...........................	− .241	− .192	.010
	− .254	− .146	− .069
Ii............................	− .289	− .357	.153
	− .180	− .297	.153
Gs...........................	− .019	− .216	.238
	.025	− .144	.193
SGI..........................	.185	− .071	.253
	.209	.005	.190
GI − SI.....................	.164	− .071	.233
	......	......	......
OI − SI.....................	.016	− .032	.057
	......	......	......
SG − OG....................	− .034	− .074	.062
	......	......	......
Extremes....................	− .077	− .159	.132
	......	......	......

The upper coefficient in each cell is obtained from "Total Deviation" scores, the lower from "Number-of-Question Deviation" scores. Data: 102 Form A papers. P.E.'s range from .067 to .059.

Deviation" scores to be more reliable, are sufficient justification for the use of these scores, even though they are somewhat less easy to obtain.

It is pertinent at this point to inquire whether the relationships between the SOGI scores and our criteria are linear. It is conceivable that for some of the characteristics thought to be measured by the SOGI Scale, people at the extremes of the distribution are more alike than different. A score in which nonlinear relationship with the measure of academic efficiency might be expected is the GI − SI. Two persons whose GI − SI scores are very different—one, say, − 50; the other +120—may really be much alike in that both are to some extent handicapped in making the most of their ability, the one by fear of failure, the other by overconfidence. Application of the Zeta Test for linearity [29 : 210] to all of the Form A data, shows $\frac{\text{Zeta}}{\text{P.E. Zeta}}$ to be in this instance but 2.10, which is not large enough to be reliable. In other words, the relationship between efficiency scores and GI − SI appears to be linear. Similar tests applied to the SG and SI scores yield similar results. In no case is the relationship found to be definitely nonlinear.

The study thus far indicates that although the SOGI Scale scores are of very satisfactory reliability, their validity for predicting academic marks directly, or indirectly through efficiency scores, is uniformly low, in nearly every instance including zero within the P.E. limits. A few scores, however, appear to have promise. Moreover, a test correlating zero with a criterion may be of distinct value in raising prediction from a multiple regression equation if its intercorrelations with the other variables used are right, as Hull has pointed out [40 : 453]. Hence, the interrelationships between the various scores are important and will be examined in some detail before an attempt is made to develop the equation for predicting academic success.

CHAPTER VII

INTERPRETATION OF RELATIONSHIPS EXISTING
BETWEEN SOGI SCORES

When all the intercorrelations between the different scores have been computed, there results Table VI, which shows the interrelationships between not only the SOGI Scale scores but the variables of marks, intelligence, efficiency, semester hours of academic work completed, and age, as well. In examining these relationships, the limitations of the data and the lack of objective validation must be kept in mind. Although these coefficients were computed from but 102 cases, these have been shown to be a true sample of all the 457 Form A papers. Without objective validation we cannot be sure that a high score on any of the SOGI variables corresponds to a high degree of emotional maladjustment. But we can, for example, say with assurance that a high score on a certain variable is related to the intelligence score of the individual to a certain degree, or is unrelated to the score on some other variable being studied. Such findings, as checked by further studies, may be expected to throw new light on the complex tangle of factors which go to make up personality.

There should first be noted the fact that spurious correlation affects certain coefficients found. This applies to the relationships of variables GI − SI, OI − SI, and SG − OG, with either of the Individual scores involved in deriving these scores. Take, for example, the GI − SI score and its correlations with GI and SI, respectively. These are found to be .633 and − .533. The tendency for GI scores to be larger than SI scores is well known, and is found in our data. Therefore, the GI − SI score of one whose GI score was large would quite probably be positive and reasonably large, while a low GI score would usually be accompanied by a still lower SI score, making the resulting GI − SI score still positive, though small. The negative relationship between SI and GI − SI may be similarly accounted for; and the same line of argument may be applied to the other two derived scores, OI − SI and SG − OG.

A further spuriously high relationship is found between GI − SI

TABLE VI

INTERCORRELATIONS OF ALL VARIABLES

Numbers of Variables	1	2	3	4	5	6	7	8	9	10	11	12	13	14	15	16	17	18
0	.539	.252	.029	.238	−.177	.026	−.137	.019	−.127	.059	−.241	−.289	−.019	.164	.016	−.034	−.077	.185
1		−.670	−.095	−.050	−.245	−.124	−.006	−.100	−.043	−.078	−.192	−.357	−.216	−.071	−.032	−.074	−.159	−.071
2			.121	.264	.145	.184	−.096	.149	−.042	.169	.010	.153	.238	.233	.057	.062	.132	.253
3				.042	−.048	−.156	−.050	−.135	.124	.013	−.151	.093	−.011	.058	.255	−.080	−.047	.007
4					.006	.162	−.038	−.004	−.142	.179	.005	.066	.115	.190	−.132	.170	.146	.199
5						.410	.280	.545	.547	.272	.344	.299	.353	.014	.416	−.154	−.006	−.003
6							.076	.756	.099	.732	.441	.468	.771	.576	.025	.438	.207	.603
7								.118	.783	.297	.442	.296	.116	−.533	−.288	−.027	−.226	−.474
8									.294	.551	.328	.352	.606	−.383	.269	−.244	.089	.407
9										−.357	.320	.233	.169	−.317	.347	−.243	−.305	−.289
10											.320	.387	.711	.633	.079	.324	−.003	.664
11												.649	.535	−.089	−.147	.230	.171	−.050
12													.646	.088	−.113	.220	.206	.119
13														.510	.059	.308	.065	.528
14															.296	.306	.175	.974
15																−.356	−.116	.244
16																	.172	.319
17																		.142

Data: 102 Form A papers. P.E.'s range from .003 to .067.

KEY TO NUMBERS OF VARIABLES

0 — Marks	8 — OG	16 — SG — OG
1 — Intelligence	9 — OI	17 — Extremes
2 — Efficiency	10 — GI	18 — SGI
3 — Hours completed	11 — Ss	
4 — Age	12 — Ii	
5 — SO	13 — Gs	
6 — SG	14 — GI — SI	
7 — SI	15 — OI — SI	

and the SGI scores. These two sets of scores, though found by somewhat different methods, can vary only slightly from each other. The first named does not take account of direction of deviation from the ideal, while the second does; but in practice the differences this makes are negligible. Very probably, then, since the SGI score is so nearly like the GI — SI, there is found spuriously high relationship between it and GI and SI, so that these relatively high coefficients, .664 and — .474 respectively, must also be discounted; and between SGI and SG, since a person with few SG differences would almost certainly have a low SGI score. With these exceptions, the sizes of the scores are determined by so many different factors that they may for practical purposes be said to be independent.

Taking the SOGI scores in turn, then, a number of observations may be made. In interpreting the relationships obtained, the size of the P.E.'s must be kept in mind. In general, with this sampling, no correlations smaller than .25 can be considered as certainly indicative of relationship.

A. Resemblance Between S and O Columns

It has been noted that the Self-Ordinary-Ideal Scale as used in this study included a fourth, or "O" column, in addition to the usual S, G, and I columns. We may now inquire how much the inclusion of this O column adds to the value of the scale. We notice first that $r_{SG:OG}$ and $r_{SI:OI}$ are high and very similar. This perhaps indicates that these two pairs of scores measure much the same factors of personality. Is this borne out by further examination? We find that though OG tends to correlate lower with other factors than does SG, e. g., $r_{OG:GI} = .551$; $r_{SG:GI} = .732$; and $r_{OG:Ss} = .328$; $r_{SG:Ss} = .441$, in all, six coefficients are lower for OG than for SG, and four are higher. On the whole, the differences between these pairs of correlations are not great, varying from .042 (SI) to .244 (OI — SI), the average difference being .150. Further evidence as to the similarity between the SG and OG scores is found by comparing their correlations with the three criteria. Here we find, with marks, intelligence, and efficiency, respectively, SG correlations of .026, — .124, and .184; and OG correlations of .019, — .100, and .149.

Examining similarly the SI and OI coefficients, we find that here there is a rather definite tendency for those of the OI scores to be higher than those of the SI, this being true of seven out of nine coefficients. Again, however, the differences are mainly small, the range being from .023 (SG) to .267 (SO), with a mean difference of but .113. The signs are without exception alike. Comparing the coefficients of these two variables with the criteria, we find again marked resemblance, these being, respectively, —.137, —.006, and —.096 for the SI, and —.127, —.043, and —.042 for the OI scores.

Finally, we note from Table III that SG and OG have means and sigmas much alike—.63.72, 61.27 for means, and 29.91, 27.30 for sigmas; and that SI and OI are likewise similar in these measures, though not so much so—64.22, and 78.72 for means, and 25.87, and 26.36 for sigmas.

We consider next the SO scores themselves, and the related Three-column Scores, OI — SI and SG — OG. The SO scores have the smallest mean, 42.26, of any of the six Individual scores, indicating that these persons tended to rate themselves as not greatly misunderstood. There is comparatively little variation in this, since the S.D. is likewise the smallest, 22.15, of the six Individual scores. The distribution is remarkably symmetrical except for a few cases which scatter out at the high end. Scores higher than 80 in SO may be considered unusual. (It should be remembered that a score of as high as 530 is possible on this score, though it would probably never be found.) An item study of SO deviations would be interesting to reveal activities on which people typically consider themselves misjudged, but as this has no bearing on the present problem it is not included here.

The OI — SI scores present clearly the tendency for the S and O columns to resemble each other. Here the mean is but +14.22, with an S.D. of 16.25. The distribution is reasonably symmetrical. Though again it is theoretically possible that the scores may vary from —530 to +530, the actual range is confined within the general limits —20 to +50, with a noticeable tendency for the individual to judge himself more leniently than he thinks others judge him. That is, he tends to consider himself somewhat misunderstood to his own disadvantage; or, to put it still differently, to rate himself more nearly all right than he feels he is generally thought to be. Though this tendency is not extreme, it is clearly present. The correlation of .416 between this score and SO is but to be expected. Neither this nor the SO score is significantly correlated with academic success, however; though we may still assume that extreme scores, beyond the range of our sampling, might be significant.

The mean of +2.16 on the SG — OG scores may be taken to indicate that though most persons tend to rate themselves as slightly more different from the group than they believe their friends think them, the difference is very small. Again, the distribution is fairly symmetrical, and its S.D. of 18.52 indicates a considerable amount of individual variation. But again, the range of scores, −40 to +30 except for the tails of the distribution, is small as compared with the possible range of −530 to +530. It is interesting to find the correlation between this score and SO insignificant (−.154). Though again scores do not correlate significantly with the criteria, it may be considered possible that extreme scores would affect academic success.

Having thus examined the scores obtained from the S column, comparing them with the scores obtained from the O column and finding such close resemblances throughout, we may conclude that the inclusion of the O column in the scale adds little to the information obtained, while adding a fourth to the taking time and doubling the scoring time if all of the Individual scores are to be used. True, certain of the scores made possible by the O column afford interesting glimpses into the probable relationships existing between various habit systems of personality, but they are none of them of practical value to the scale for our present prognostic purposes. In a revised form this O column should be discarded (see page 73).

B. Intercorrelations of SI Scores

The strong tendency noted by Knight and Franzen [46] of persons to rate others as further from the ideal than they rate themselves is corroborated here in a comparison of the means of the SI and GI scores, which are 64.22 and 83.24, respectively. Examining the correlations of the first of these, we note first the coefficient of .442 with Ss, which seems to indicate a noticeable tendency for persons with large differences between self and ideal to have also peculiar interests. Peculiar interests rather than peculiar ideals seem to go with self-ideal differences, since the correlation between SI and Ii is but .296. The absence of correlation (.076) between SI and SG is somewhat surprising. Though we usually picture the person with large self-ideal difference as judging himself different from the group, this evidence indicates that no relationship exists. Again, the SI scores are not closely akin to group-ideal difference, there being found only a low correlation (.297). Unfortunately, we can get no direct information as to the relation between SI scores and probable superiority-inferiority because of the spurious correlation existing. But though we cannot rely entirely on the SI: (GI − SI) and SI: SGI coefficients which were found, the two scores in each case do vary with enough independence to make it safe to assume that a true negative relationship exists, even though we cannot be sure of its amount. That is, a high SI score tells us little about the size of the accompanying GI score, and accordingly tells us still less about the resulting GI − SI score. The same may be said of the SI and SGI scores. We may conclude, then, that persons with high SI scores tend to have low SGI and GI − SI scores, which presumably means that a large amount of self-ideal difference is likely to be accompanied by feelings of inferiority. Only where both scores are at the extremes of the distribution can we expect this to represent a serious enough condition to be likely to affect academic success noticeably.

C. Intercorrelations of OI Scores

Passing next to the OI scores, we find that the individual who has a high OI score (i. e., who says that others judge him far from what he feels would be ideal) is very likely to have a large self-ideal difference, but also is apt to have a large SO ("misunderstood") score. He may have any degree of SG or Gs difference, which indicates that one's judgments regarding himself and his relation to his ideal have very little connection with his feeling of "at homeness" in his group or his ability to understand the group. He tends slightly to feel inferior (negative correlations with GI − SI and SGI), and is apt to have somewhat unusual interests and ideals. The individual with a high SI score presents a very similar picture, it may be noted, except that he is not so likely to have a high SO score. It is of interest to observe that these two scores, OI and SI, yield the highest correlations with the Extremes scores. There is a low but consistent tendency for persons with high OI or SI scores to be cautious in their ratings ($r_{\text{OI: Ext.}} = -.305$; $r_{\text{SI: Ext.}} = -.226$). One hypothesis regarding this finding would be that these persons tend to be introvertive, since the introvert is notably careful in contrast to the more impulsive extravert. No facts on this hypothesis are available at present.

D. Intercorrelations of GI Scores

When we examine the relationships of GI, we note at once the strong tendency for persons with large GI differences to have also large SG differences. This is in keeping with the previous finding that people usually rate S nearer I than they rate G. That is, the mean GI score,

as has been said, is higher than the mean SI score.   The similarity of
the SG and SI means (63.72 and 64.22, respectively) indicates that as
a rule persons tend to rate themselves about midway between their
rating of the group and their rating of the ideal.   The high correlation between SG and GI (.732) indicates that S tends to vary with I,
or to resemble it, and this is borne out by the relatively low correlation
(.297) between SI and GI, and by the fact that both GI and SG
scores correlate similarly with Gs and OG.   Here, as GI becomes
larger, S tends to follow I, thus increasing SG.   This tendency is
notably more marked than that for S to follow G, since that would
make SI increase as GI does, whereas $r_{GI:SI}$, as has been said, is but
.297.   The high correlations of SG and GI with OG suggest that
persons with large self-group or group-ideal differences tend strongly
to rate themselves thought of as standing out from the group.   We
may note further in this connection that the OG scores throughout
correlate markedly with scores that may be measures of superiority:
thus, $r_{OG:Gs} = .606$; $r_{OG:SGI} = .407$; $r_{OG:(GI-SI)} = .383$; but, as was mentioned above, its correlations with these variables are lower than are
those of SG.   The higher correlation of OG with SG (.756) than with
SO (.545) suggests that persons who judge that others think they are
different from the group are more apt to do so because they feel themselves to be different than because they think they are misjudged by
others.   The difference in coefficients is not, however, large enough for
a great deal to be made of this tendency.   The lack of relationship between the GI and the OI − SI scores is striking.
Apparently harshness of self-judgment and harshness of group-
judgment vary independently, so that the degree of severity
with which a person judges himself is no criterion of the severity with
which he will judge the group.   There is some tendency for those
who judge the group harshly to have peculiar ideals ($r_{GI:II} = .387$)
and to have peculiar interests ($r_{GI:Ss} = .320$).   This might have been
expected.   The correlation of .324 between GI and SG − OG is in
keeping with this finding.

E. Intercorrelations of Ss and Ii Scores

We examine next the Ss scores.   Here it appears that persons
with peculiar interests usually have peculiar ideals; that they tend to
be out of close contact with the group, since $r_{Ss:SG} = .441$ and $r_{Ss:Gs} = .535$; and that they are apt to be persons with large SI scores.
Peculiarity of interest is apparently unrelated to superiority-

inferiority; and its relationships with SO, OG, OI, GI, and SG — OG are low but uniformly positive.

The Ii scores, peculiarity of ideal, present a closely similar picture. The notable fact about both of these Group-Individual scores is that a high degree of peculiarity, either of interest or of ideal, constitutes the greatest handicap to good academic work of any of our scores. True, the correlations are not high, being respectively —.241 and —.289, but they seem to indicate a relationship, and a negative one at that. Presumably the explanation is that a peculiar set of interests or ideals indicates an individualistic person, who tends to work well enough at what interests him, but to be bored with all else. In higher education he finds many required tasks which are often distasteful, and against these he rebels, securing in consequence somewhat lower marks than would be expected. It may be pointed out that this finding that good students tend to have interests and ideals which conform rather closely to those of the group as a whole (i. e., to have low peculiarity scores) is in general corroboration of Morris's discovery [61 : 28] that "the reactions of the strong teachers are more sharply defined than those of the weak." On a like-dislike questionnaire of interests she found 63 teachers who were rated as strong varying less in their responses than 52 teachers rated as weak. Our data indicate that good students tend to have lower peculiarity of interest and peculiarity of ideal scores than do poorer students.

The negative relationship between the Ss and Ii scores and intelligence is startling. Though the correlation of —.192 between Ss and intelligence is not significant, that of —.357 between Ii and intelligence is. Does it indicate that there is a noticeable tendency for the less intelligent person to develop peculiar ideals, while the more intelligent person is satisfied to let his ideals conform to those of the majority of his associates? Shall it be taken to mean that more intelligent persons are in general better adjusted to the realities of life than are those of less intelligence? A host of other interpretations might be suggested, each rich in possibilities for moralizing, but the true explanation of this finding will have to await further experimentation in this field.

F. INTERCORRELATIONS OF Gs SCORES

The Gs score is interestingly related to the measures of probable superiority-inferiority and to the scores expressing feelings of difference. Thus, the person who makes a high Gs score tends to have high SG ($r=.771$), high OG ($r=.606$), high GI ($r=.711$), high Ss ($r=.535$), high Ii ($r=.646$), high GI $-$ SI ($r=.510$), and high SGI ($r=.528$) scores. It is hard to escape the conclusion that large self-group and group-ideal differences, a strong tendency to rate the group further from the ideal than one rates oneself, and highly individualistic interests and ideals give us a picture of "superiority." This indicates that "superiority" and inaccurate judgment of the group often go together. It does not tell us which is the cause of the other. But since the Gs distribution is markedly skewed toward the top, 56 per cent of the cases falling within the lowest fifth of the total range, while those of "superiority" (GI $-$ SI and SGI) are more nearly normal, it is clear that some people who have high "superiority" scores do make low Gs scores; i. e., though people who are poor judges of the group usually consider themselves as superior, not all who rate themselves as superior are poor judges of the group. Further investigation makes it apparent that we cannot call the Gs score a measure of superiority, for if we compare in turn the correlations with various other scores of Gs with the correlations of those same scores with GI $-$ SI and SGI, we shall find considerable differences. GI $-$ SI and SGI, however, correlate almost identically, as would be expected.

Although the Gs score is thus hardly to be thought of as a measure of superiority, it is clearly a measure of ability to judge correctly the interests of the group. In this connection it is reasonable to find that persons with large OG scores tend to have large Gs scores also. That is, their idea that they appear to stand out from the group is due in part to lack of clear insight into the actual attitudes of the group. The same may be said of the high correlation between Gs and SG. If these individuals could be brought to a clearer understanding of group likes and dislikes, they might find themselves more like others than they now believe. It is true, however, that such people do tend to have peculiar interests and ideals ($r_{Gs:Ss} = .535$ and $r_{Gs:Ii} = .646$). Hence for some persons with high OG and SG scores, at any rate, their idea of themselves as "different" is largely justified.

G. Intercorrelations of Extremes Score

The Extremes score has already been mentioned. With the exception of its low, but significant, correlations with OI and SI, its relationships with the other SOGI scores are of negligible importance, as are likewise those with the criteria. It tells us little of value about personality, and is of no use in predicting academic success.

CHAPTER VIII

DIFFERENCES IN SOGI SCORES BETWEEN VARIOUS GROUPS

Before any decision can be reached as to the predictive value of the SOGI Scale, it is necessary to know how stable an instrument it is. That is, do marked fluctuations in its scores exist between various groups of students? We shall need to know whether significant sex differences are found, and whether graduate and undergraduate groups differ noticeably; lastly, we may inquire whether departmental groups are so unlike as to affect the predictive value of the scale. If such differences are found, separate regression equations will be needed for each of the various groups to be used. We shall, therefore, study these groups to ascertain whether significant differences exist among them.

A. Sex Differences

Other tests of emotional adjustment have found it necessary to develop separate norms for men and women. Representative of these are the Colgate Tests of Emotional Outlets and the Allports' study of Ascendance-Submission. The first of these, using the same test for both sexes, gives different norms. A recent study by Broom [6] finds, however, "no appreciable sex differences in extraversion and introversion as measured by the Laird [Colgate] test, C_2." The second test uses separate forms for men and women. Do significant sex differences in SOGI scores exist in the data of the present study?

To get at the facts most efficiently, all scores from the SOGI Scale were T-scaled. This made it possible to combine the three forms, giving larger numbers and smaller standard errors. The difference of means technique was employed throughout. The criterion factors, and hours and age, as well as twelve of the fourteen SOGI scores, were included in the study. SGI and Extremes were omitted, the first because of its resemblance to $GI - SI$, the second because of its lack of value. In order to avoid confusing differences due to academic status with sex differences, the study was confined to the graduate students. A sex difference study of undergraduates was impractical, there being but to undergraduate men's papers in all the data. For the graduates, the numbers were satisfactory, there being a total of 210 men's papers and 589 women's papers. From the calculations on these two groups, Table VII results.

TABLE VII

Sex Differences of All Variables: Graduate Men and Graduate Women, All Forms

Scores (* = T units)	M.A. Men (N = 210)		M.A. Women (N = 589)		Diff. S.D. Diff.	Chances in 100
	Mean	S.D.	Mean	S.D.		
Marks *	51.49	6.98	51.60	6.14	.20	58
Intelligence *	53.38	8.96	51.60	7.62	2.58	99.5
Efficiency	98.70	7.72	100.47	7.57	2.90	99.8
Hours	13.37	3.27	14.12	2.85	2.88	99.8
Age	32.23	7.74	31.79	7.60	.72	76
SO *	52.61	9.61	50.66	9.49˙	2.53	99.4
SG *	50.47	10.08	50.21	9.45	.33	63
SI *	48.26	9.42	50.94	9.51	3.53	100 +
OG *	50.34	10.59	50.41	9.53	.08	53
OI *	50.06	10.34	50.74	9.53	.84	80
GI *	51.36	9.84	50.60	9.67	.96	83
Ss *	50.16	9.82	50.17	9.63	.01	50
Ii *	52.34	9.81	50.12	9.86	2.81	99.7
Gs *	51.86	10.23	50.50	9.81	1.68	96
GI − SI *	52.84	9.96	50.20	9.58	3.34	100 +
SG − OG *	51.07	10.59	49.84	9.51	1.48	93
OI − SI *	52.26	10.53	50.22	9.93	2.43	99.3

From this table we note that the only statistically reliable sex differences in the SOGI scores are in SI and GI − SI. Women have greater amount of self-ideal difference than do men, and make lower GI − SI scores. This is in agreement with the finding of Heidbreder [35] that women show more "inferiority," according to both self

ratings and those of associates, than do men. Considering scores
whose $\frac{\text{Diff.}}{\text{S.D. Diff.}}$ approaches 3.00, we find the men making higher SO,
OI — SI, and Ii scores. That is, men appear to think themselves
more misjudged than do women, and to have more peculiar, i.e.,
more individualistic, ideals than do the latter. Though the group
norm used in obtaining the Ii scores for the men was obtained from
the mixed sampling of 102 papers which included but 14 men's papers,
it has already been shown in Chapter IV that the scores for men
obtained in this way agree almost perfectly with those obtained from
a norm derived from all the men's papers. Hence this sex difference
in Ii scores is probably a true one.

No difference in marks is found between the sexes, though the men
are almost certainly of greater intelligence and carry lighter academic
loads. The women are, therefore, found to use nonintellectual factors
more profitably than the men do, thus making up for their lower
intelligence and heavier loads. No age difference of any significance
is found.

B. ACADEMIC STATUS DIFFERENCES

We next inquire what differences due to academic status exist in
the factors we are studying. In what respects are undergraduates
different from graduate students? Using the same technique as
before, and considering only the undergraduate and graduate women,
in order to avoid confusion with sex differences, we have Table VIII.

If we consider only those differences which are statistically reliable,
the SOGI scores are eliminated at once. This means that in developing regression equations, academic status may be neglected so far as
the SOGI scores are concerned. Age similarly fails to show a significant difference. Though such difference as is present indicates that
the undergraduate women are older, this is undoubtedly a chance
occurrence. On the other four factors the differences are reliable.
The graduate women make higher marks and are more intelligent than
the undergraduates, but the latter carry more hours of academic
work and bring to bear more successfully the various nonintellectual
factors than do the graduates. Graduation, as would be expected, is
found to act as a selective agent, the more intelligent, on the whole,
returning for further study. The higher marks of these graduate
students are accounted for partly by their superior ability, and partly
because their academic load is lighter than the undergraduates.

TABLE VIII

ACADEMIC STATUS DIFFERENCES OF ALL VARIABLES: UNDERGRADUATE AND
GRADUATE WOMEN, ALL FORMS

SCORES (* = T units)	B.S. Women (*N* = 530)		M.A. Women (*N* = 589)		DIFF. S.D. Diff.	CHANCES IN 100
	Mean	S.D.	Mean	S.D.		
Marks *.............	49.58	6.21	51.60	6.14	5.46	100 +
Intelligence *........	48.14	7.40	51.60	7.62	7.69	100 +
Efficiency...........	102.35	6.56	100.47	7.57	4.48	100 +
Hours...............	14.85	2.83	14.12	2.85	4.29	100 +
Age.................	32.55	7.12	31.79	7.60	1.73	96
SO *...............	50.22	10.02	50.66	9.49	.76	77
SG *...............	50.02	9.84	50.21	9.45	.33	63
SI *...............	50.68	9.93	50.94	9.51	.45	67
OG *...............	49.74	10.04	50.41	9.53	1.14	87
OI *...............	50.34	10.20	50.74	9.53	.68	75
GI *...............	50.31	10.12	50.60	9.67	.48	68
Ss *...............	50.70	9.81	50.17	9.63	.90	82
Ii *...............	50.32	9.66	50.12	9.86	.34	64
Gs *...............	50.12	9.84	50.50	9.81	.64	74
GI − SI *..........	50.25	9.78	50.20	9.58	.09	54
SG − OG *..........	50.85	9.90	49.84	9.51	1.74	96
OI − SI *..........	49.82	9.46	50.22	9.93	.69	76

C. DEPARTMENTAL DIFFERENCES

Finally, we investigate possible differences between students of different departments of instruction. It should be noted at the outset that at the institution from which our data were drawn, departmental divisions are not emphasized, and there is great overlapping of courses between students of all departments. Nevertheless, in the graduate school, students are classified by departments of major interest, and it is therefore pertinent to ask whether a student's scores on the SOGI Scale are affected by the department of his choice, and whether students in one department seem better adjusted than those in others. If marked differences should be found, this fact would need consideration in developing regression equations for prediction of academic success.

It is interesting to wonder whether such differences as may be found exist because persons working in a given department develop similar interests and prejudices and the like, or because persons with similar interests, prejudices, and the like choose the same department in which to work. Little data in answer to this query can be brought to bear in this study, since we have no information as to length of time spent in a department. If working in a given department produces a certain amount of bias, we should expect this to increase with length of stay. Our Ph.D. candidates would thus show more diversity between departments than our M.A. candidates. But the paucity of cases at this higher level makes impossible such a comparison, since there are but 95 papers of Ph.D. candidates in all our data, and these are distributed among a number of departments. Further, there seems less reason to expect departmental differences in the various self-attitudes that we are studying than in the degrees of interest in various activities which persons say they possess; and these latter are not under investigation here.

A serious limiting factor in any departmental difference study with our present data is the fact that we have in few departments enough cases to give any sort of picture of those departments. The undergraduate papers are eliminated at the outset, since those students pursue a general course. The papers of graduate students embrace twenty-two departments, and when they are divided by sex, the numbers available within either sex for a comparative study become disappointingly small. We ought to have at least fifty papers from one sex as a basis for each department studied. There are, however, but two departments which have fifty or more women's papers, and none with fifty men's papers. If we lower the limit to forty, we include the women's papers of five departments. There are still no men's papers included. We must content ourselves, then, with a study of departmental differences shown by the women of the following five departments:

> Department 2—Advisers
> Department 4—English
> Department 11—Psychology
> Department 17—Household Arts
> Department 21—Physical Education

Although department 22, Education, has enough cases to justify its inclusion, it is omitted because it does not represent a stabilized course in which relatively homogeneous groups might be expected.

The groups established, we now study the distributions of scores for the five departments. Statistical measures of these are given in Table IX, and the reliabilities of differences found are given in Table X.

By adding the differences found between each pair of departments compared, and ranking them by amount of difference found, we get (Table X) a rough measure of the degrees of resemblance between departments. It appears from this that departments 4 and 17 are

TABLE IX

Statistical Measures of Variables for Certain Departments, All Forms

SCORES (* = T Units)	DEPT. 2 (N = 47)		DEPT. 4 (N = 53)		DEPT. 11 (N = 40)		DEPT. 17 (N = 99)		DEPT. 21 (N = 46)	
	Mean	S.D.	Mean	S.D.	Mean	S.D.	Mean	S.D.	Mean	S.D.
Marks *	51.74	6.53	50.85	6.37	52.80	6.31	50.02	5.66	51.82	5.55
Intelligence *	54.00	7.36	53.38	6.12	53.40	8.96	47.58	6.76	50.87	7.77
Efficiency	98.21	6.41	98.00	6.38	99.75	7.35	102.83	7.04	101.56	8.06
Hours	13.72	2.74	12.52	2.74	14.28	3.11	15.03	2.48	15.02	2.15
Age	32.06	6.01	29.85	5.99	29.00	8.21	31.22	6.12	28.30	4.97
SO *	50.76	8.99	53.04	8.35	49.83	10.18	49.50	10.11	48.94	10.20
SG *	48.46	7.46	52.52	9.54	51.78	10.53	48.89	10.55	48.02	8.77
SI *	50.05	11.28	54.08	9.63	49.60	10.65	49.98	9.66	49.13	6.76
OG *	48.52	7.81	53.85	10.26	50.50	9.65	49.01	10.28	48.48	8.76
OI *	49.73	10.35	53.15	10.52	49.75	9.98	47.89	10.68	49.52	6.85
GI *	48.97	8.84	51.36	11.32	51.70	10.19	50.17	10.16	47.89	7.80
Ss *	50.24	10.56	52.46	9.56	50.50	11.67	50.89	8.91	48.28	8.77
Ii *	49.29	9.00	50.85	10.16	48.55	10.61	50.89	8.92	49.65	8.50
Gs *	47.88	9.44	51.88	11.13	51.10	10.56	50.08	8.50	49.98	7.49
GI − SI *	49.29	8.61	48.65	9.93	52.90	9.93	49.56	9.82	48.74	8.49
SG − OG *	49.35	9.36	48.42	11.55	51.02	8.85	50.32	8.54	49.58	9.57
OI − SI *	49.22	9.80	50.15	10.66	51.18	9.87	49.80	10.00	50.89	8.52

most alike, with 4 and 21 a close second. At the other extreme, 2
and 11, 11 and 21, and 2 and 21 resemble each other closely. English
appears to be the most unique department; Advisers, Psychology,
and Physical Education resemble each other markedly; Household
Arts stands about midway between English on the one hand and the
other three departments on the other.

TABLE X

DEPARTMENTAL DIFFERENCES, EXPRESSED IN S.D. Diff. UNITS

Derived from data of Table IX

SCORES	DEPARTMENTS COMPARED									
	2, 4	2, 11	2, 17	2, 21	4, 11	4, 17	4, 21	11, 17	11, 21	17, 21
Marks..........	.69	.77	1.55	.06	1.47	.79	.81	2.42	.76	1.80
Intelligence.......	.53	.34	5.06	2.05	.07	5.23	1.70	3.70	1.39	2.47
Efficiency........	.16	1.17	3.91	2.20	1.34	4.27	2.40	2.12	.97	.91
Hours...........	2.19	.89	2.79	2.55	2.84	5.46	5.00	1.36	1.28	.02
Age.............	1.83	1.95	.78	3.30	.55	1.33	1.40	1.54	.47	3.08
SO.............	1.30	.45	.76	.92	1.62	2.30	2.16	.17	.40	.31
SG.............	2.37	1.67	.28	.26	.35	2.15	2.45	1.46	1.78	.52
SI.............	1.88	.19	.04	.48	2.09	2.48	2.98	.20	.24	.61
OG.............	2.93	1.04	.32	.02	1.61	2.76	2.80	.81	1.01	.32
OI.............	1.63	.01	1.00	.12	1.58	2.91	2.04	.97	.12	1.11
GI.............	1.18	1.37	.73	.62	.15	.64	1.78	.80	1.92	1.48
Ss.............	1.09	.11	.37	.98	.87	.98	2.26	.19	.99	1.66
Ii.............	.81	.35	1.01	.20	1.05	.02	.64	1.22	.53	.81
Gs.............	1.93	1.48	1.36	1.19	.34	1.02	1.00	.54	.56	.07
GI − SI.........	.34	1.80	.17	.31	2.03	.54	.05	1.80	2.07	.52
SG − OG........	.44	.86	.60	.12	1.22	1.04	.49	.43	.72	.45
OI − SI.........	.45	.92	.33	.88	.48	.20	.38	.75	.14	.68
Sum of differences.	21.75	15.37	21.06	16.26	19.66	34.12	30.34	20.48	15.35	16.82
Rank, by amount of difference....	3	9	4	8	6	1	2	5	10	7

The differences found may be conveniently summed up under two headings: A, those which are certainly reliable, i. e., in which the $\frac{\text{Diff.}}{\text{S.D. Diff.}}$ is 3.00 or more; and B, those which are very probably reliable, i. e., in which the $\frac{\text{Diff.}}{\text{S.D. Diff.}}$ is between 2.00 and 2.99. Table XI presents these findings. It will be seen that the differences between departments are not great, at most, since between the most unlike departments, 4 and 17, there are but three significant differences out of the seventeen factors studied. The lack of differences in marks is explained by the fact that the average mark of each student is obtained from class marks made in various departmental courses.

Not a single surely significant difference is found between these departments on any of the 12 SOGI scores studied, though in a number of instances the chances of a real difference approach certainty. The

TABLE XI

SUMMARY OF CERTAIN AND PROBABLE DIFFERENCES BETWEEN DEPARTMENTS STUDIED

Based on Data of Table X

DEPARTMENTS COMPARED	A. CERTAIN DIFFERENCES $\frac{\text{Diff.}}{\text{S.D. Diff.}} = 3.00$ or more	B. PROBABLE DIFFERENCES $\frac{\text{Diff.}}{\text{S.D. Diff.}} = 2.00$ to 2.99
2 and 4	None	2, lower SG and OG scores 4, fewer hours
2 and 11	None	None
2 and 17	2, lower efficiency scores 17, lower intelligence scores	2, fewer hours
2 and 21	21, younger	2, lower efficiency scores, fewer hours 21, lower intelligence scores
4 and 11	None	4, lower GI − SI scores and fewer hours 11, lower SI scores
4 and 17	4, lower efficiency scores, fewer hours 17, lower intelligence scores	17, lower SO, SG, SI, OG, and OI scores
4 and 21	4, fewer hours	4, lower efficiency scores 21, lower SO, SG, SI, OG, OI, and Ss scores
11 and 17	17, lower intelligence scores	11, lower efficiency scores 17, lower marks
11 and 21	None	21, lower GI − SI scores
17 and 21	21, younger	17, lower intelligence scores

resemblances or differences between departments on these scores follow in general their resemblance or lack of it on other factors; thus, 2 and 11, the departments most alike, show small differences on most of the SOGI scores, while 4 and 17, most unlike, show large differences on nearly all. But that the SOGI scores do not go together uniformly will be seen at once if the differences of the two pairs of departments just mentioned are examined critically. Though for 2 and 11 most of the differences are small, the range is from .01 to 1.80; though for 4 and 17 most of the figures are large, the range is from .02 to 2.91. This fact, as well as the low intercorrelations found between certain scores, indicates that the scores measure different aspects of personality.

Since the departmental differences are, on the whole, so small, and for the SOGI scores in every case not significant, it will not be advisable, with the small number of cases at our disposal, to try to develop separate regression equations for different departments. Departmental differences will therefore be ignored in our predictions of academic success. Sex and academic status do make enough difference, however, in certain of the factors which are included in our predictive battery, to make it wise to develop through further research more refined predicting instruments than the equation presented in the next chapter.

CHAPTER IX

PREDICTIVE POWER OF SOGI SCALE

Although no one of the scores from the SOGI Scale correlates highly with academic marks, it may well be that several of them, properly combined and weighted, will be of appreciable value. Our next concern then becomes finding out which scores are of greatest value for use in a multiple regression equation with marks as the criterion. This is the heart of the problem under investigation. Unless it can be shown that the use of certain scores from the SOGI Scale in conjunction with intelligence scores and other measures easily obtained, such as age, results in a substantially better prediction of academic success than is obtained by predicting from intelligence scores alone, we must conclude that the SOGI Scale is of no value for our present purpose. Although there is no real limit to the number of variables which may be used in building the regression equation, it is obviously desirable that they be as few in number as is consistent with a high multiple correlation. To develop directly an equation that would incorporate all eighteen variables to predict the criterion would entail an almost endless amount of labor, much of which would be of no practical value since it can be determined by other means which variables will contribute significantly to the total predictive value of the equation. In order to select these important variables from the total battery, the method set forth by Hull [40 : 450] is convenient. We desire:

1. that when the correlations between the criterion, marks, and each of two scores are both large and of the same sign, the correlation between these scores be as low (i. e., as near −1.00) as possible;

2. that when the correlations between the criterion and two scores are large, but one correlates positively with the criterion and the other negatively, the correlation between the two scores be as high (i. e., as near +1.00) as possible;

3. that when the correlation between the criterion and one score is large, and that between the criterion and another score is

zero, the correlation between the two scores be as large (i. e., as far from .oo) as possible, regardless of sign.

With these guiding principles before us, we first examine in Table VI the row of coefficients of the variables with the criterion.   Numbers 4, 5, 11, 12, 14, and 18 correlate .15 or more here, which correlation, though low, presumably indicates relationship.   Further examination reveals the fact that of these six scores, the following intercorrelations are low 4 : 5, .006; 4 : 11, .005; 4 : 12, .066; 5 : 14, .014; 5 : 18, −.003; 11 : 14, −.089; 11 : 18, −.050; 12 : 14, .088.   Moreover, since variable 1 will surely be included in the final battery, we must note which of these six scores give low intercorrelations with 1.   The following are found: 1 : 4, −.050; 1 : 14, −.071; 1 : 18, −.071.

Looking in detail at the correlations of variable 4 with these others, we find undesirably high correlations with scores 14 and 18.   Accordingly, we examine these in turn.   Scores 14 and 18 are themselves almost perfectly correlated, due to the fact that their values, though derived in different ways, are of necessity practically identical.   One or the other must be discarded.   Although 18 correlates a trifle higher with the criterion, it is so much more difficult to score accurately that its practical value is dubious.   Accordingly, we decide in favor of 14.   Variable 4 is retained, though its correlation of .190 with 14 is objectionable.

Variable 5 is found to correlate almost zero with 14, but much too highly with 11 and 12.   It can be used only if 11 and 12 are discarded. Since 11 and 12 intercorrelate .649, one must be discarded anyway. Though the difference in their respective correlations with 14, and its higher correlation with the criterion incline us to favor 12 (Principle 2, above), we decide finally for 11 because of its much smaller negative correlation (and hence "higher," in Hull's sense) with 1, which more than outweighs the other considerations.

We have now to decide between 5 and 11, an easy matter, since 11 correlates more highly with the criterion.   Thus far, then, the significant variables are 4, 11, 14, and, of course, 1.

Next we examine the scores correlating practically zero with the criterion, to see if any have high correlations with variables that correlate highly with the criterion.   Scores 3, 6, 8, 10, 13, 15, 16, and 17 have near-zero correlations with marks.   Examining in turn the correlations of these with our significant variables, 1, 4, 11, and 14, we find 3, 15, 16, and 17 to have such low correlations as to be useless.

6 is of fair promise, 8 scarcely usable, 10 is about on a par with 6. This leaves 13 as the most promising addition to our battery, and the other variables are therefore discarded.

The final battery of scores for predictive purposes, then, contains variables 1, 4, 11, 13, and 14. Three of these are scores from the SOGI Scale: 11 is Ss, "peculiarity of interest"; 13 is Gs, "insight"; and 14 is GI − SI, "superiority." Variable 1 is intelligence, and 4 is age.

We have now to determine the regression equation and the co-efficient of multiple correlation, R, of this test battery. The first of these will give the respective weights to be assigned to the variables in predicting the most probable marks which a student will make; the second tells how good the prediction is, i.e., how well such predicted marks correspond to marks actually made. Using the method detailed by Hull [40: 457], we find the regression equation to be:

$$X_0 = .4183X_1 + .1848X_4 - .2146X_{11} + .1086X_{13} + .0527X_{14} + 2.9288.$$

The coefficient of multiple correlation is:

$$R_{0(1, 4, 11, 13, 14)} = .6413 \pm .0393.$$

How much better is prediction from this equation than from intelligence scores alone? The coefficient of alienation, k, which is equal to the expression $\sqrt{1 - r^2}$, will tell us this. Where r is .539, k is .8423; for $R = .641$, $k = .7675$. That is to say, using intelligence scores alone as a basis for predicting marks, our prediction is but 15.77 per cent better than pure chance (since pure chance is represented by a k of 1.0000). The use of the multiple regression equation above makes prediction 23.25 per cent better than chance. This is a gain in "forecasting efficiency" of 47.4 per cent. According to Hull, few batteries in use to-day give predictions more than 30 per cent better than chance; therefore our equation appears to be of considerable value.

There is still, however, a large error of prediction. The standard error of estimate for the multiple regression equation is 4.59, which may be compared with that of 5.04 if intelligence scores alone are used. In the latter case we may say of a predicted marks score that the chances are 68 out of 100 that the marks actually obtained will lie within a range of ±5.04 from the predicted score. With predictions from the multiple equation this range shrinks to ±4.59.

We may be practically certain that a score will be found actually to lie within the limits of ± 3.00 S.D.est. from the score predicted. This means that if we predict a marks score of 50 on the basis of intelligence score alone, we may be practically certain that the individual in question will obtain a marks score between 34.88 and 65.12. If we predict a score of 50 on the basis of the multiple regression equation just developed, our range of practical certainty is confined within the limits of 36.23 and 63.77. Since for practical prediction, decimals would be dropped, this means that the use of the SOGI Scale has narrowed the range of practical certainty by only one point at each extreme. The range is still great enough to include everything from a C— to an A— average, according to studies of Teachers College grades made by Spence [75 : 55] and Krieger [48 : 28]; and in terms of letter grades the multiple regression equation tells us no more than prediction from intelligence alone.

We may now ask how great a part in raising the multiple correlation is played by the various tests and scores used. The pertinent figures showing the multiple correlation obtained by the use of intelligence scores alone and in various combinations with the other scores, are given below:

VARIABLES	VALUE OF R	KEY TO NUMBERS OF VARIABLES
o (1)	.539	o = marks
o (1, 4)	.601	1 = intelligence
o (1, 11)	.557	4 = age
o (1, 13)	.548	11 = Ss
o (1, 14)	.576	13 = Gs
o (1, 4, 11)	.617	14 = GI — SI
o (1, 4, 13)	.605	
o (1, 4, 14)	.620	
o (1, 11, 13)	.592	
o (1, 11, 14)	.588	
o (1, 13, 14)	.576	
o (1, 4, 11, 13)	.639	
o (1, 4, 11, 14)	.632	
o (1, 11, 13, 14)	.597	
o (1, 4, 11, 13, 14)	.641	

A critical examination of these relationships reveals several important facts.

1. Variable 14 added to the other variables increases the R by but .002. The forecasting efficiency of the battery without variable 14 is 23.08 per cent. Obviously, this score, GI — SI, adds so little as to make its use with the other 4 variables unnecessary.

2. An R of .620, representing forecasting efficiency of 21.54 per cent, is secured by the use of variable 14 with variables 1 and 4. Evidently, the GI — SI score has value, but not in conjunction with Ss and Gs.

3. The R is raised from .539 to .601, and the forecasting efficiency improved 27.4 per cent by simply including the variable age with intelligence scores.

4. The total contribution of the SOGI scores, when combined in a multiple regression equation with intelligence scores and age in years to predict marks, is represented by the difference between a forecasting efficiency of 23.08 per cent and 20.08 per cent, a gain of 3 per cent. Stated differently, prediction from intelligence and age is 27.4 per cent better than from intelligence alone; prediction from intelligence, age, and Ss and Gs scores is 46.4 per cent better than from intelligence alone; and if GI — SI scores be added, the gain in prediction is 47.4 per cent over intelligence alone. It is thus apparent that the maximum contribution of the SOGI scores here used is a trifle less than that of age in determining academic success in the institution from which these data were drawn.

When we use only the Ss and Gs scores from the SOGI Scale, and the variables of intelligence and age, the multiple regression equation becomes:

$$X_0 = .4183X_1 + .1891X_4 - .2425X_{11} + .1382X_{13} + 3.4090.$$

This, when used to but two places for practical work, gives a multiple correlation with marks of .64, $\pm$.0394 and has a standard error of estimate of 4.60.

In interpreting the foregoing increases in prediction, the probable errors of the coefficients must be kept in mind. The P.E. of .539 is .0474; that of .64 is .0394. In the construction of the equation some coefficients not certainly representative of the true relationships involved have been used. Therefore the resulting multiple correlation is probable rather than certain. The regression equation has not been developed for the entire body of data studied for two reasons.

1. Since the sample of 102 Form A cases has been shown (Chapter IV) truly representative of all the data of that form, greater reliance may be placed on the findings than would be true if these cases stood alone. They represent 457 cases.

2. Since the SOGI scores improve prediction no more than they are here found to do, improvement in the prediction of academic success is to be sought along other lines than through the use of the SOGI Scale unless (*a*) further research should develop as yet untried ways of scoring the Scale, or (*b*) unless items more valid for the prediction of academic success can be discovered and standardized for a new form of the SOGI Scale.

CHAPTER X

DIFFERENTIATING POWER OF ITEMS USED IN PRESENT FORMS OF SOGI SCALE

Further improvement in ability to predict academic success seems to involve primarily improvement in ability to measure adequately the various "nonintellectual" factors which go to determine an individual's efficiency score. As it stands, Form A of the SOGI Scale is of no practical value for the prediction of efficiency, the correlations of its various scores with efficiency all including zero within the ± 4 P.E. range. It is, however, possible that certain items may possess value for differentiating between persons whose efficiency scores will be high and those whose efficiency scores will be low, but their value is at present hidden or canceled by other items either not differential or differential in the opposite direction.

That the test as it stands possesses little differentiating power may be shown by a comparison of the distributions of scores of two groups, representing the extremes of high efficiency and low efficiency—high efficiency students having marks T scores higher than their intelligence T scores, with resulting efficiency scores above 100; low efficiency students having marks T scores lower than their intelligence T scores, with resulting efficiency scores below 100. Taking the two extreme groups, we have approximately 50 papers of each form in each group, as shown below, representing for the high group all the women with efficiency scores of 109 and up, and for the low group all the women with efficiency scores of 92 and down.

FORM	PAPERS IN HIGH GROUP	PAPERS IN LOW GROUP
A	59	51
B	46	41
C	51	46

The men's papers were eliminated to avoid sex differences, and could not be dealt with separately because of the small number of cases available.

When the two sets of distributions are compared by the difference of means technique already used in previous chapters, the results are as shown in Table XII. The short formula is here used. From this table we note that, as is usually found, those with high efficiency scores are less intelligent than those with low efficiency scores, but that in spite of this apparent handicap, they make significantly better marks than do the low efficiency students. These differences are probably largely spurious, due to the nature of the efficiency scores and to the relationship existing between marks and intelligence, as Toops and Symonds [83] have pointed out. That the high efficiency group completes a significantly greater number of academic hours than does the low efficiency group is but another indication that this group has better study habits and other factors which are not

TABLE XII

COMPARISON OF HIGH AND LOW EFFICIENCY WOMEN ON ALL VARIABLES—
ALL FORMS

SCORES (* = T scores)	HIGH EFFICIENCY N = 156		LOW EFFICIENCY N = 138		DIFF. S.D. DIFF.	CHANCES IN 100
	Mean	S.D.	Mean	S.D.		
Marks *........	53.76	5.72	47.13	6.32	9.34	100 +
Intelligence *....	41.73	5.41	58.59	6.30	24.41	100 +
Hours..........	14.82	2.76	13.41	3.30	3.92	100 +
Age............	33.36	7.42	30.38	8.01	3.31	100 +
SO *..........	50.35	10.05	49.96	9.80	.34	64
SG *..........	50.02	10.28	50.30	9.12	.25	60
SI *..........	49.79	10.27	51.61	9.06	1.62	94
OG *..........	49.73	10.34	49.91	9.71	.15	56
OI *..........	50.21	10.94	50.37	9.38	.13	55
GI *..........	50.90	10.88	50.78	9.87	.10	54
Ss *..........	51.13	9.48	49.59	8.87	1.44	93
Ii *..........	52.84	9.82	49.44	9.98	2.96	99.9
Gs *..........	51.27	9.66	50.20	9.98	.93	83
GI − SI *......	51.48	10.02	49.61	9.63	1.63	94

measured by the intelligence tests, but which affect marks. Their greater age suggests that these factors are learned, i. e., that as those who remain in collegiate work grow older, they tend to become better oriented, to learn "the tricks of the trade."

Turning to the scores of the SOGI Scale, we find no surely significant differences between the two groups. Four of the scores yield differences represented by 90 chances or more out of 100, however. Surveying these, we find that the high group tends to have lower SI scores and higher Ss, Ii, and GI — SI scores. If our interpretation of these scores is correct, this means that a small amount of self-ideal difference, together with peculiar interests, peculiar ideals, and freedom from inferiority, tend to go with high achievement relative to one's intelligence. The picture presented here seems to be that of the individualistic person, who goes his own way with little regard for custom, and who feels reasonably well satisfied with himself. However, it is to be remembered that both Ss and Ii showed negative correlations with intelligence. High scores on these factors among persons of high efficiency may be explained in part by the fact that these persons are of lower average intelligence than the low efficiency group.

In order to ascertain whether certain items were of greater differentiating value than others, an item study was next made from these same papers, representing for each form the extremes of the efficiency distribution. For each of the items of each form, tabulations were made of the distribution of responses on each of the six Individual "Total Deviation" scores—SO, SG, SI, OG, OI, and GI, for high and low groups separately. It was then possible to examine the responses to any item, comparing tendencies of high and low groups. In general, the distributions were not greatly different, but some showed a marked tendency for, say, the high group to have many responses of no deviation, while the low group had fewer. Since a comparison of each successive step of deviation for each item would have involved a refinement of technique not warranted by the somewhat small number of cases, it was thought advisable simply to compare for each item the percentage of zero deviation with the percentage of deviation of one or more. Borrowing and adapting a technique reported by Chambers [10] with the Pressey X O Tests, any item was considered differential if there was a difference of 10 per cent or more between the deviation responses of the high and low groups on that item.

There were, it will be recalled, 109 items in all: 28 in Form A, 28 in Form B, 28 in Form C, and 25 comprising the last part of all forms.

For each item, then, there were found the percentage of the high group showing deviation, the percentage of the low group showing deviation, and the difference between these percentages. This was done for all six Individual "Total Deviation" scores. It was hoped at first that there could thus be found some fifty items which were satisfactorily differential on each of the six scores. But the tabulation showed that though an item might be very differential for one score or even for two or three, it seldom was for more, and never for all six. Further, many items showed differentiating ability in opposing directions on various scores. Thus, item 25A showed the following percentage differences, where plus means a higher per cent of deviations in the high group and minus, a higher per cent of deviations in the low group: SO, +18; SG, +4; SI, −18; OG, −5; OI, +4; GI, +7. This was undesirable, because if the "Total Deviation" scores of a new form were to correlate significantly with the efficiency scores, the individual items must be, so far as possible, differential in one direction. Which direction made little difference, and might be chosen by inspection of the data, but it must be uniform. Actual inspection showed that there were more items on which the low group showed a higher percentage of deviation than the reverse—that is, more minus than plus differences. This is seen in Table XIII, in which all differences of 10 per cent or more are shown. It will be noted that some of the items showed no differences this large. It is also to be noted that the last twenty-five items show fewer differences than the other items do. These are not quite fairly represented in the table, however, for since they are common to all forms, the N for both high and low groups was substantially three times that of the first twenty-eight items. Accordingly, such differences as are found are much more likely to be reliable.

It is recognized that for any item the statistical significance of the differentiation depends not alone on the amount of percentage difference, but also on the actual per cents of deviation and no deviation in both high and low groups. Study to ascertain which items showed certainly reliable differentiation indicated that for the first half of each form, where the N was relatively small, differences even as large as 20 per cent were not always reliable; and for the last half, with its larger N, differences of less than about 15 per cent were seldom reliable. (For the formula used for this study, see Yule [95 : 269].) To have used only differences certainly reliable in developing a differential scoring unit would have given far too few responses to be of

TABLE XIII

SUMMARY OF DIFFERENCES BETWEEN HIGH AND LOW EFFICIENCY WOMEN IN PERCENTAGE OF DEVIATION RESPONSES FOR THE SIX INDIVIDUAL TOTAL DEVIATION SCORES. ONLY DIFFERENCES OF 10 PER CENT OR MORE ARE SHOWN

First Half of Scale

ITEM	FORM A						FORM B						FORM C						TOTALS
	SO	SG	SI	OG	OI	GI	SO	SG	SI	OG	OI	GI	SO	SG	SI	OG	OI	GI	
1	11																		
2			−16	−14				22	−12				−12				−20		
3	19		−27	−14				−11	−17								−13		
4			−14	−16	−10					−15	−15	10						−13	
5	12		−13	16	20				−27		−12	−15		15	−17				
6					16			−15		−10	−12		−26		−22			−13	
7			−26	12	12			−23			−18	−15						−10	
8			−14					−26											
9							17					−15	13	−10	20	−15			
10	16	20	−17	12	12	22	−10						10	17	13	−40	12		
11		12	11	11	17			−22	−31	−15		−15	10			14	−14		
12	14		−12	−14	19	17		−16	−16	−11	−19	−21	−19	−12	−12	−15	12		
13					−10				−15		−18	11	−24	10		−11	12	−16	
14								−17	−18	−26	−17	−17	−15			16	−14	23	
15				14				−11	−15	−12			−23		23	−17	−16	−11	
16	10		−15		22				−15	−16	11	−10	−20		−15	−21	−18		
17		12	10					−16			−18	−13			20		−10		
18				11	21	−10	20		−12			12		11			−15	−11	
19	24	13	−16	−16				19		−19		13		−10	12	−21	−19		
20	18		−18	13					11	−22		19	−15	−13				−11	
21			11						−16	12									
22			−14						−25	−15									

Last Half of Scale

ITEM	ALL FORMS						TOTALS
	SO	SG	SI	OG	OI	GI	
29						10	
30							
31							
32							
33	−11	−14					
34							
35				−10	−12		
36				−10	−10		
37							
38	−11						
39							
40							
41				−12			
42	11	−11					
43							
44							
45							
46				−10			
47							
48			−17			−13	
49							
50						14	
51						11	
52							
53							

Totals

	FORM A						FORM B						FORM C						TOTALS		ALL FORMS						TOTALS
	SO	SG	SI	OG	OI	GI	SO	SG	SI	OG	OI	GI	SO	SG	SI	OG	OI	GI			SO	SG	SI	OG	OI	GI	
Total plus	7	5	2	8	8	2	2	3	1	1	5	5	5	4	6	2	3	1	70		1	2	5	1	1	3	4
Total minus			12	4	2	2	1	11	12	10	6	6	8	3	7	9	6	4	103		2	2	5	1	1		11
Total	7	5	14	12	10	4	3	14	13	11	11	11	13	7	13	11	9	5	173		3	2	5	1	1	3	15

Plus differences indicate a higher percentage of deviations of one or more in the high efficiency group; minus differences, a higher percentage of deviation in the low efficiency group. The table is read as follows: Item 1, Form A, shows only one difference as large as 10 per cent; this is found in the SO score, and the high efficiency group have more deviations than the low efficiency group by 11 per cent. Item 1, Form B, shows a difference of 13 per cent in the OI score, the high group again having the larger percentage. Item 1, Form C, in the OI score shows 20 per cent more of the low efficiency group to have had deviations than of the high group.

practical value. Hence the 10 per cent differentiation was arbitrarily used. It gave, as will be seen from Table XIII, a total of 188 differential points.

In theory, a test made up of items found to be differential as between high and low efficiency groups should yield scores that would correlate highly with actual efficiency. The predicted efficiency score, considered with the intelligence score of the individual, would then make possible a reasonably accurate prediction as to the academic standing that this person would probably achieve. If his intelligence is low, it will take a higher probable efficiency score to bring him within the realm of "good risks," academically speaking, than will be needed if his intelligence is higher and his predicted efficiency score is still positive. Conversely, mere high intelligence will not insure desirability, for if accompanied by a low enough probable efficiency score, the student may be considered a probable "loafer." We may now inquire whether the differential scoring plan used on our present data will show a significant correlation with efficiency scores.

To answer this query, a scoring key for Form A was prepared from Table XIII. This showed each item in Form A which was differential and the direction of differentiation. The supposition is that each time a person has a deviation response where the high group had one, or has none where they had none, he is showing a tendency to be like them; and that if on this basis he makes a high score (counting one point for each likeness) he may be expected to have a high efficiency score. The total number of points possible in Form A was 67, items 1–28 furnishing 52 of these points, and items 29–53 the remainder.

The Form A papers of all the women, both B.S. and M.A. candidates, whose efficiency scores were between 93 and 108 inclusive, were now scored with this key, and the correlation between these predicted efficiency scores and the actual efficiency scores was computed. It proved to be but .05±.041. The reliability of these scores, calculated by the odd-even method and corrected by the Prophecy Formula, proved to be .28±.039, which is perhaps as high as could be expected, since many of the differential items used did not themselves represent a reliable difference between high and low efficiency groups. Greater reliability would doubtless have been secured had it been possible to use only those items which differentiated to the extent of 20 per cent or more, although, as has been noted, not all of even these are reliable. There were, however, but 31 of these in all three forms, so that this was impossible. Again, a slightly higher correlation between predicted and actual scores would doubtless have been secured had it been possible to include in the papers scored by this plan the extremes of the actual efficiency distribution; but this could not be done because all of the extreme papers had been used in building up the score card, in order to secure greater numbers.

We may well give some attention to the items in which these 31 scores that differentiate to the extent of 20 per cent or more between high and low efficiency groups are found. Although, as will be seen in Table XIV, few of these possess a reliability that is practically certain (i.e., a $\frac{\text{Diff.}}{\text{S.D. Diff.}}$ of 2.78 or more), a number of them approach it. They may throw some light on the "efficient personality" versus the "inefficient personality" from the standpoint of making the best use for academic purposes of ability possessed. The 31 scores in this class occur in 24 test items, there being 7 of these items having two differential scores each.

If now we interpret each of the six Individual "Total Deviation" scores investigated here as indicating, roughly, a "sore spot" or source of more or less disturbance, we may draw from Table XIV a general picture of the "inefficient personality." First, we note that the inefficient person is more apt than is the efficient person to make deviation responses, 19, or 61 per cent, of these 31 differential scores showing more deviations in the low group than in the high. Incidentally, this is the same percentage found in Table XIII, where out of a total of 188 responses differential by 10 per cent or more, 114, or 61 per cent, showed more deviations in the low group. Next, we note that the inefficient group give numerous indications of poor general adjustment. Thus, they appear disturbed over such matters as "always being on time for your engagements" (27B), "being well thought of by your associates" (7B), "being well dressed" (13B), "finding new inspiration" (6C), "being a mystic" (12C), "being consistent" (18C), and the like. These seem to indicate a person of introspective, sensitive tendencies, who spends considerable time in wondering what sort of impression he is making, how well he is succeeding, etc. The efficient group, on the other hand, appears to find its chief sources of deviation or disturbance from such items as "working with people who talk very slowly" (16A), "people who talk very fast" (11C), "witty people" (10A), "funny stories" (23A), "dull children" (23B), "going to the movies" (19C), etc. These suggest the less introspective type of person, though their disturb-

TABLE XIV

RELIABILITY OF DIFFERENTIATION BETWEEN HIGH AND LOW EFFICIENCY WOMEN OF ITEMS 20 PER CENT OR MORE DIFFERENTIAL

ITEM NUMBER	ITEM	SCORES DIFFER-ENTIAL	PER CENT HAVING DEVIATIONS OF 1 OR MORE		DIFF. S.D. DIFF.	CHANCES IN 100
			High Group	Low Group		
3A	Meeting people from other parts of U. S.	SI	45	72	2.99	99.9
6A	Working with people who talk very slowly	OI	80	60	2.32	99
7A	Working with a person who is intensely interested in getting some particular thing done	SI	41	67	2.83	99.7
10A	Witty people	SG GI	78 66	58 44	2.28 2.37	98.9 99.1
19A	Being able to read one or more foreign languages	OI	88	66	2.80	99.7
23A	Funny stories	SO OI	48 75	24 54	2.72 2.34	99.7 99
2B	Gaining the respect of your pupils	SG	68	46	2.12	98
7B	Being well thought of by your associates	SG SI	45 44	68 71	2.22 2.65	98.6 99.6
9B	Securing better salaries for teachers	SG	50	76	2.62	99.5
13B	Being well dressed	SG SI	54 41	76 72	2.22 3.07	98.6 100 +
15B	Doing things that will provide real thrills	GI	67	88	2.44	99.3
16B	Going to social functions like dances, bridge parties, teas, etc.	OG	62	88	2.96	99.9
23B	Dull children	SO	50	30	1.95	97.5
25B	More liberal immigration laws	OG	40	62	2.10	98
27B	Always being on time for your engagements	SI	41	66	2.42	99.2
1C	Having someone else assume responsibility in important affairs	OI	71	91	2.62	99.5
6C	Finding new inspiration	SO SI	44 54	70 76	2.68 2.34	99.7 99
11C	People who talk very fast	SI	76	56	2.11	98
12C	Being a mystic	OG	38	78	4.38	100 +
18C	Being consistent	SO	41	65	2.44	99.3
19C	Going to the movies	SI OI	76 80	53 57	2.42 2.50	99.2 99.4
21C	Doing each job in the best possible way	SO	38	61	2.33	99
22C	Getting settled in some place or job	OG SO	55 37	76 57	2.24 2.01	98.7 98
23C	Being obeyed	SI	67	47	2.02	98

This table is read as follows: In Item 3A, which was "meeting people from other parts of the U. S.," the SI score was found differential to the extent of 20 per cent or more. Here 45 per cent of the high efficiency group showed deviation responses, and 72 per cent of the low efficiency group showed deviation responses. The difference in per cents is 2.99 times the S.D. Diff. There are 99.9 chances in 100 that this is a reliable difference. The remaining lines are read similarly.

ances over "gaining the respect of your pupils" (2B), and "being obeyed" (23C) seem to be exceptions. In the main, however, it is felt that these findings bear out the assumption that academic efficiency may be impaired by emotional disturbances. Krieger [48 : 61] obtained further evidence of this fact when she sent questionnaires to some of the same students whose tests we are studying here, and found 47 per cent of the "inefficient" group and but 29 per cent of the "efficient" group reporting that they "felt handicapped in courses during the semester" (Fall, 1927). The difference shows 98.9 chances in 100 of being reliable. Among handicaps voluntarily listed were difficulty in adjustment and emotional difficulties throughout the semester.

The item study, then, has indicated clearly several facts.

1. In the SOGI Scale, as it stands, items are differential between high and low efficiency groups of students (*a*) in varying amounts, and (*b*) in opposing directions. This is one reason why the scores described in Chapter IV fail to correlate significantly with efficiency.

2. It is found that even by using items most differential as a scoring unit the correlation with efficiency remains insignificant.

3. The use of items whose differentiating power is not certainly reliable does not produce a score of sufficient reliability for individual prognosis, the coefficient being only .28 ± .039.

4. Certain items are found whose differentiating power is reliable. These give some insight into the differences between efficient and inefficient students. By further research, following leads suggested here, it seems reasonable to expect that a test for predicting efficiency can be developed which will possess adequately high reliability.

CHAPTER XI

SUGGESTIONS FOR FURTHER STUDY OF SOGI TECHNIQUE

As seems to be usual in research, this study raises for further investigation more problems than it solves. Several of these will be suggested here.

1. In the first place, since the Self-Ordinary-Ideal Rating Scale has been proved reliable, it would be desirable to discover just what relationships exist between such factors of personality as it measures and other factors for which there have already been devised measuring instruments. One would like to know, for example, how the various SOGI scores correlate with the extraversion-introversion scores of the Colgate C 2 Scale, and other attempted measures built around this concept. The writer has limited data collected for such a study, and hopes shortly to present it. Relationships between SOGI scores and those obtained from the A-S Reaction Study should also be studied.

2. Valuable for a more thorough understanding of precisely what this SOGI technique measures, would be a careful validation, through case studies, of the SOGI scores. Until such a study is made, we cannot tell whether or not a person who makes a high SG score, for example, really *feels* that he is different from other persons. It should be pointed out, however, that even should such a person be found not to feel different, he (*a*) exhibits a surprisingly stable tendency to rate himself as different, and (*b*) in this tendency he differs in degree from similar self-ratings of other persons. That is, even should case studies fail to establish the fact that a high SG score corresponds to feelings of being different, or that a minus score on GI−SI corresponds to "inferiority feelings," it remains true that these scores, reliable as they are, measure personality factors of some sort.

3. Therefore, although such case study validations would add to our knowledge about the SOGI technique, more practical use of the scale and greater advances in the more fundamental problem of the

nature of personality itself will be obtained through further studies of relationships existing between SOGI scores and objective evidences of success or failure in various types of endeavor. Of these, academic success is but one. Certain of the SOGI scores have been shown to bear low but consistent negative relationships to academic success and efficiency. What is their bearing upon such an activity as practice teaching? Upon actual teaching success? Upon popularity? Upon leadership? Upon success along various vocational lines? Careful studies of this sort are believed to be important.

4. In anticipation of further uses of the Self-Ordinary-Ideal Rating Scale, several suggestions for changes in the form are to be recommended.

A. Eliminate the O column, retaining the other three. The responses on the O column differ little in the main from the S, and none of the scores using O responses seems of especial value. Further, the four-column form takes longer both to administer and to score than does the three-column form.

B. Reduce the fineness of the response scale. As used in the present study, the scale consists of eleven points, o through 10, representing degrees of attitude from intense aversion to intense liking. Scoring of total deviations between any two columns is done item by item, the scorer noting the amount of each deviation and adding it mentally to the sum of those previously obtained until the total is reached. This method requires very close attention on the part of the person scoring, and is, therefore, slow and fatiguing. It was found that to get the six Individual "Total Deviation" scores required a minimum of four minutes per paper, even after the scorers had been trained and had had several days of practice. Though cutting out the O column would leave but three Individual Scores to be obtained instead of six, and would shorten the scoring time about half, the process would still be a fatiguing one, requiring very close and sustained attention. Further scoring ease would be gained by making the response scale less fine, using a nine- or possibly even a seven-point scale. Sweet [79], in adapting the technique for boys, uses a five-point scale scored by the "Number-of-Question Deviation" technique. Conklin [13], basing his conclusions on an analysis of some 23,000 individual judgments, found adults capable of using a scale as fine as nine points in distinguishing pleasure-displeasure or belief-disbelief. A tabulation of nearly 70,000 responses for each of two columns (S and I) of our data revealed distributions as follows:

Response	S Column Frequencies (%)	I Column Frequencies (%)
10	13.2	32.6
9	19.5	21.4
8	22.4	17.3
7	13.1	8.0
6	8.5	4.7
5	9.6	9.4
4	4.7	1.8
3	4.0	1.5
2	1.9	.9
1	2.0	1.1
0	1.1	1.3
Median response.....	8.2	9.2

Here, 91 per cent of the S responses and 95.2 per cent of the I responses are found in seven points of the eleven-point scale used. Making the scale coarser would doubtless reduce slightly the reliability of the scores, since it would approach the "Number-of-Question Deviation" type of scores; but even these averaged .73 in reliability. With the reduced scale, the mental additions in scoring would be largely in units of 1 or 2 instead of often 4 to 7 or 8 as at present, and this would obviously make for much greater scoring speed and ease as well as accuracy.

c. If using such a revised form with the regression equation given above for prediction of academic success, obtain in the following manner the scores needed:

1) After administering the scale to a group, take a random sample of exactly 100 papers and tabulate, for each item, the frequencies of each response of the scale for the S column only. From the resulting distributions determine to the nearest integer the mean for each item. These means are the group norms, designated by a small letter s. Prepare a scoring key on a strip of paper, so constructed that it can be placed vertically alongside the individual's responses.

2) To obtain Ss scores, use the group norm key laid beside the S column of the individual paper. Add deviations, neglecting direction, item by item. The sum is the Ss score.

3) To obtain Gs scores, proceed in the same manner except that the group norm key is to be compared with the individual G column.

4) Age, as here used, is simply chronological age in years.

5) If the regression equation here given were to be used, the intelligence scores should be obtained from the same tests used in this study. If other measures of intelligence are used, new regression equations should be developed.

CHAPTER XII

CONCLUSIONS

This study has concerned itself with the use of a modified form of the Self-Ordinary-Ideal Rating Scale, called here the SOGI Scale, as a measure of probable factors of individual self-attitudes as determined by the subject's responses to a paper and pencil test; and with the effect of such factors upon academic success in teacher-training courses. That the scale might be used as a measure of interests alone, and that these might be so scored as to assist in the prediction of academic success, is taken for granted because of evidence that has been presented by other investigators. No attempt to use the present data in that way has been made.

An investigation of fourteen different scores obtained in various ways from the SOGI Scale indicates that all are surprisingly reliable, the mean reliability being .85. This is sufficiently high to assure that the SOGI technique measures factors of personality which are relatively stable in individuals, though gradually changing over a period of time. Thus the scores from retests with the same items, given about seven months after the original data were secured, averaged .69 in reliability. Further, the low correlations of the SOGI scores with intelligence, averaging $-.126 \pm .067$, indicate that whatever these personality factors being measured are, they are related scarcely at all to intelligence. Only two of the fourteen SOGI scores show correlations with intelligence high enough to leave zero out of the ± 4 P.E. range, these being the SO and Ii scores. In both of these instances, the correlation with intelligence is negative, as, indeed, are the correlations obtained for all the other twelve scores. We have, then, an indication that the personality characteristics which the SOGI Scale measures tend very slightly to be found to a greater degree among persons of lower intelligence. Due to the very highly selected nature of our group, this shows up in a very limited way, and should be checked by more extended studies among a less homogeneous population, before any certain conclusion on this finding can be reached; but the probabilities are that in an unselected popula-

75

tion the negative relationship between intelligence and the SOGI scores would be greater than that found here.

The SOGI scores correlate only slightly with academic marks, only two showing correlations certainly greater than zero. These two are the Ss and Ii scores, and again, both correlations are negative. This is the direction we should expect, since common sense suggests that persons who think of themselves as someway set off or "different" in various respects from their fellows might be troubled enough by this attitude to let it interfere with their academic efforts. Here again, the limitations of our data must be noted. There were included for study the SOGI papers of only those students who had successfully completed eight or more hours of work during the semester. Thus the failing students were eliminated at the outset, and the group was made exceptionally homogeneous as to marks. A study of SOGI scores in a population less homogeneous from the standpoint of marks would presumably show larger negative correlations.

With the unfortunately restricted data here considered, it does not appear that the SOGI Scale in its present form may be used to improve to any practical extent the prediction of academic success. By the use of certain SOGI scores with intelligence scores, an R of .64 is obtained. This is a gain of nearly 50 per cent in forecasting efficiency over the correlation of .539 between intelligence and marks alone. In this regression equation the Ss and Gs scores are used from the SOGI Scale, age and intelligence being the other two variables used. The Ss scores are found to have slightly over one-half the weight of the intelligence scores for determining the predicted marks, while Gs is given about one-fourth the weight of intelligence. Age is somewhat less important than the Ss scores in this equation. The equation, carried to but two decimal places for convenience in use, is

$$X_0 = .42X_1 + .19X_4 - .24X_{11} + .14X_{13} + 3.41,$$

where
X_0 = predicted marks average T score
X_1 = intelligence T score
X_4 = age
X_{11} = Ss score
X_{13} = Gs score,

and it gives a multiple correlation of .64 ± .039, the standard error of estimate being 4.60. Its value for the practical prediction of marks is, however, but slightly better than intelligence scores alone.

The main importance of the study is felt to be not in the improvement of prediction made possible through the use of the SOGI Scale, since equally high multiple correlations have been previously obtained through other techniques. The value seems to lie largely in another direction. At the outset the assumption was made that factors of disturbed self-attitudes might exert a depressing effect upon academic success, though it was recognized that in most individuals this effect would doubtless be slight. It was further assumed that these self-attitudes might be detected and measured by the paper and pencil technique known as the Self-Ordinary-Ideal Rating Scale. These assumptions now appear to have been fully justified. The factors revealed by this scale, whatever names we may give them, are measured with highly satisfactory reliability. Though their validity for our present purpose is, in the case of most scores, of little significance, it is reliable for certain scores and uniformly in the direction expected. Thus the technique of the SOGI Scale is sound, and with further research to discover additional items of high validity, it gives promise of real value for the measurement of aspects of personality not primarily intellectual.

There seems no good *a priori* reason against believing that the validity of certain of the SOGI scores for discovering other characteristics than the likelihood of academic success may be considerably higher. Success in the academic field is conditioned by intelligence to a much greater degree than in some of the vocational and personal fields; and since the scores obtained from the SOGI Scale are but slightly related to intelligence, they may be expected to be of greater value when used for personality studies in non-academic fields. The further use and study of the Self-Ordinary-Ideal Rating Scale is therefore believed to offer distinct possibilities for advancing our ability to measure nonintellectual personality factors and our consequent knowledge and understanding of that most intricate of disciplines—human behavior.

APPENDIX

SAMPLE COPIES OF SOGI FORMS USED IN THIS STUDY*

Name.........................

GENERAL EXAMINATION—PART V

Write your identification number here...............

Time-1 Hour

Below is a scale by which one may indicate degrees of interest in various activities, persons, or things.   Following the scale is a list of items, the interest in which you are to evaluate in four different ways.   Consider the first item and then place in the columns at the right four numbers which seem to best indicate the appropriate degrees of interest.   Then do the next one and so on until you have finished. Do not spend too much time on any item.   Apportion your time.   This is not the sort of test where there is one best answer.   Each person will have his own scale of values.

1. In the column headed S (Subjective), indicate *your interest* in each of the following activities, persons, or things by writing the number which stands for the appropriate degree of interest.

2. In the column headed O (Objective), indicate *the interest which you think other people feel you have* in each of the items.   You may be doubtful about the value to assign in some cases, but make the best evaluation you can.

3. In the column headed G (Group), indicate *the interest which you think characterizes the average person in your group.*   Try to think of your major professional group.   If you are an elementary school teacher, think of the average elementary school teacher; if you are a school superintendent, think of the average superintendent; etc.   Make the best estimate you can of the average interest of your group.

4. In the column headed I (Ideal), indicate *the interest which you think ideally, if you were perfect, you would possess.*

SCALE

10. Tremendously, passionately interested in and favorable towards.
9. Very much interested in, apt to enjoy it markedly.
8. Considerably interested, favorable.
7. Mildly interested, favorable.
6. Very slightly interested, favorable.
5. Quite indifferent, neutral, passive.

* Devised by Dr. Goodwin B. Watson and Dr. Ralph B. Spence and included with their permission.

79

4. Very slightly inclined to dislike, oppose, be afraid.
3. Somewhat inclined to dislike, oppose.
2. Considerably disliking, opposing, afraid of.
1. Very much inclined to dislike, oppose, be repulsed by.
0. Tremendously, passionately opposed to, repulsed by, afraid of.

(1927—1928)

A	S	O	G	I	
Making money..........................					1
Learning to think more clearly..............					2
Meeting people from other parts of the United States...............................					3
Helping to bring about the abolition of wars.....					4
Seeing that wrong doers get their proper punishment...........................					5
Working with people who talk very slowly......					6
Working with a person who is intensely interested in getting some particular thing done.........					7
Learning new things about your job...........					8
Having a friend that you can feel really understands you...........................					9
Witty people..............................					10
People who insist on taking charge of things.....					11
Developing a sense of humor.................					12
Providing for your father and mother..........					13
People more intelligent than you are..........					14
Bright children............................					15
Taking an active part in church work.........					16
Being well versed in the field of art...........					17
Doing your job as well as or better than anyone else in your group........................					18
Being able to read one or more foreign languages					19
Teaching a class...........................					20
Making school more interesting for children.....					21
Insisting that those over whom you have charge fulfill all your requirements................					22
Funny stories.............................					23
Listening to grand opera....................					24
Differing in opinion with someone else.........					25
Playing practical jokes.....................					26
Taking part in vigorous physical exercise.......					27
Doing tasks that require more than usual patience					28
Taking responsibility in important affairs.......					29
Adults over forty..........................					30
Developing more respect for law and order in pupils..................................					31
Meeting new people........................					32
Children from two to five years of age.........					33

	S	O	G	I	
Creating international mindedness............					34
Becoming more open minded.................					35
Trying out new ways of doing things..........					36
Adolescent children.......................					37
Inspiring your pupils......................					38
Working out a more satisfying philosophy of life.					39
Befriending someone that no one else takes an interest in...............................					40
Telling the truth..........................					41
Children from six to twelve years of age........					42
People from other countries.................					43
Doing routine tasks........................					44
People who always agree with you............					45
Doing things that will be regarded as a permanently great achievement...................					46
Adults under forty........................					47
Doing something different from what your associates expect of you........................					48
Methodical people.........................					49
Breaking free from social tradition and customs..					50
Emotional people..........................					51
Giving teachers more freedom in determining what and how they shall teach.............					52
People who are slow in making decisions........					53

B	S	O	G	I	
Reading humorous magazines................					1
Gaining the respect of your pupils............					2
Helping to decrease political grafting..........					3
Finding pupils' felt needs...................					4
Belonging to organizations like the Rotary, Elks, Eastern Star, Women's Club, etc...........					5
Children who are always into mischief.........					6
Being well thought of by your associates........					7
Conceited people..........................					8
Securing better salaries for teachers...........					9
Being able to speak before an audience.........					10
People who always argue....................					11
Reading poetry...........................					12
Being well dressed.........................					13
Cautious people..........................					14
Doing things that will provide real thrills.......					15
Going to social functions like dances, bridge parties, teas, etc..........................					16
People who always want to tell others of their troubles.................................					17

	S	O	G	I	
Attaining better physical vigor................					18
Moulding the character of those with whom you associate.................................					19
People less intelligent than yourself...........					20
Doing each task just well enough to meet the need					21
Stricter censorship of books and plays.........					22
Dull children..............................					23
Finding more than one solution for a problem...					24
More liberal immigration laws................					25
Becoming less inclined to worry over little things					26
Always being on time for your engagements.....					27
Improving your memory.....................					28
Taking responsibility in important affairs.......					29
Adults over forty...........................					30
Developing more respect for law and order in pupils..................................					31
Meeting new people.........................					32
Children from two to five years of age.........					33
Creating international mindedness.............					34
Becoming more open minded.................					35
Trying out new ways of doing things...........					36
Adolescent children.........................					37
Inspiring your pupils........................					38
Working out a more satisfying philosophy of life					39
Befriending someone that no one else takes an interest in...............................					40
Telling the truth............................					41
Children from six to twelve years of age........					42
People from other countries...................					43
Doing routine tasks.........................					44
People who always agree with you.............					45
Doing things that will be regarded as a permanently great achievement..................					46
Adults under forty..........................					47
Doing something different from what your associates expect of you......................					48
Methodical people..........................					49
Breaking free from social tradition and customs..					50
Emotional people...........................					51
Giving teachers more freedom in determining what and how they shall teach.............					52
People who are slow in making decisions........					53

C

	S	O	G	I	
Having someone else assume responsibility in important affairs..........................					1
Being impartial to all pupils...................					2
Being allowed to tend to your own affairs without interference............................					3
Trying out new theories of education...........					4
Developing a professional spirit among educators					5
Finding new inspiration......................					6
Reading professional magazines................					7
Bringing about a better condition of social equality in this country....................					8
Quick tempered people......................					9
Publishing an article in some magazine.........					10
People who talk very fast.....................					11
Being a mystic..............................					12
Being well read in contemporary literature......					13
People who can't take a joke..................					14
Marking papers.............................					15
Thrifty people..............................					16
A person who will never make a decision if he can avoid it.................................					17
Being consistent............................					18
Going to the movies.........................					19
Energetic people............................					20
Doing each job in the best possible way........					21
Getting settled in some place or job...........					22
Being obeyed...............................					23
Watching athletic contests...................					24
Taking smart pupils down a peg...............					25
Stricter parental control for children under 18...					26
Keeping accurate and careful records..........					27
Having a keen intellect......................					28
Taking responsibility in important affairs.......					29
Adults over forty...........................					30
Developing more respect for law and order in pupils..................................					31
Meeting new people.........................					32
Children from two to five years of age.........					33
Creating international mindedness.............					34
Becoming more open minded..................					35
Trying out new ways of doing things...........					36
Adolescent children.........................					37
Inspiring your pupils........................					38
Working out a more satisfying philosophy of life.					39
Befriending someone that no one else takes an interest in...............................					40

	S	O	G	I	
Telling the truth............................					41
Children from six to twelve years of age........					42
People from other countries..................					43
Doing routine tasks.........................					44
People who always agree with you............					45
Doing things that will be regarded as a permanently great achievement..................					46
Adults under forty..........................					47
Doing something different from what your associates expect of you........................					48
Methodical people..........................					49
Breaking free from social tradition and customs'.					50
Emotional people...........................					51
Giving teachers more freedom in determining what and how they shall teach..............					52
People who are slow in making decisions........					53

BIBLIOGRAPHY

Because of the extensive bibliographies of measures of personality and character which are already available (see references 51, 52, 56, 57, 66, 90, 91), only references of which actual mention is made in the text are included here.

1. ALLPORT, G. W. A Test for Ascendance-Submission. *Journal of Abnormal and Social Psychology*, 1928, 23, 118–136.
2. ALLPORT, G. W. AND ALLPORT, F. H. *The A-S Reaction Study: a Scale for Measuring Ascendance-Submission in Personality.* Boston: Houghton Mifflin, 1928. Pp. 15.
3. ANDERSON, J. E. AND SPENCER, L. T. The Predictive Value of the Yale Classification Tests. *School and Society*, 1926, 24, 305–312.
4. BENDER, I. E. Ascendance-Submission in Relation to Certain Other Factors in Personality. *Journal of Abnormal and Social Psychology*, 1928, 23, 137–143.
5. BRIDGES, J. W. AND DOLLINGER, V. M. The Correlation Between Interests and Abilities in College Courses. *Psychological Review*, 1920, 27, 308–314.
6. BROOM, M. EUSTACE. A Critical Study of a Test of Extroversion-Introversion Traits. *Journal of Juvenile Research*, 1929, 13, 104–123.
7. BROWN, W. M. *Character Traits as Factors in Intelligence Test Performances.* Archives of Psychology, No. 65, 1923. Pp. 65.
8. BURTT, H. E. Measuring Interest Objectively. *School and Society*, 1923, 17, 444–448.
9. BURWELL, W. R. AND MACPHAIL, A. H. Some Practical Results of Psychological Testing at Brown University. *School and Society*, 1925, 22, 48–56.
10. CHAMBERS, O. R. Character Trait Tests and the Prognosis of College Achievement. *Journal of Abnormal and Social Psychology*, 1925, 20, 303–311.
11. CHARTERS, W. W. Success, Personality, and Intelligence. *Journal of Educational Research*, 1925, 11, 169–176.
12. COGAN, L. C., CONKLIN, A. M., AND HOLLINGWORTH, H. L. An Experimental Study of Self-Analysis, Estimates of Associates, and the Results of Tests. *School and Society*, 1915, 2, 171–179.
13. CONKLIN, EDMUND S. *The Scale of Values Method for Studies in Genetic Psychology.* University of Oregon Publications, 1923. Pp. 36.
14. COWDERY, K. M. Measurement of Professional Attitudes. *Journal of Personnel Research*, 1926, 5, 131–141.
15. CRANE, ESTHER. An Investigation of Three Plans for Selecting the Students to be Admitted to College. *Journal of Educational Psychology*, 1926, 17, 322–330.
16. DORCUS, R. M. Some Factors Involved in Judging Personal Characteristics. *Journal of Applied Psychology*, 1926, 10, 502–518.
17. EARLE, MARY G. The Relation Between Personality and Character Traits and Intelligence. *Journal of Applied Psychology*, 1926, 10, 453–461.
18. FILTER, R. O. An Experimental Study of Character Traits. *Journal of Applied Psychology*, 1921, 5, 297–317.

19. FRANZEN, RAYMOND. Measurement of Non-Intellectual Aspects of Behavior. *Proceedings of First Annual Conference on Educational Research and Guidance,* San Jose Teachers College Bulletin, California, 1922.

20. FRETWELL, E. K. *A Study in Educational Prognosis.* Contributions to Education, Number 99, Teachers College. 1917.

21. FREYD, MAX. The Measurement of Interests in Vocational Selection. *Journal of Personnel Research,* 1922, 1, 319–328.

22. FREYD, MAX. A Method for the Study of Vocational Interests. *Journal of Applied Psychology,* 1922, 6, 243–254.

23. FREYD, MAX. Introverts and Extroverts. *Psychological Review,* 1924, 31, 74–87.

24. FRYER, DOUGLASS. The Significance of Interest for Vocational Prognosis. *Mental Hygiene,* 1924, 8, 466–505.

25. FRYER, DOUGLASS. Interests and Abilities in Educational Guidance. *Journal of Educational Research,* 1927, 16, 27–39.

26. FRYER, DOUGLASS. Predicting Abilities from Interests. *Journal of Applied Psychology,* 1927, 11, 212–225.

27. FURFEY, P. H. *The Measurement of Developmental Age.* Educational Research Bulletin, Catholic University of America, 1927, II, 10.

28. GARRETT, H. E. Personality as "Habit Organization." *Journal of Abnormal and Social Psychology,* 1926, 21, 250–255.

29. GARRETT, H. E. *Statistics in Psychology and Education.* New York: Longmans, Green and Company, 1926. Pp. xiii, 317.

30. GILLILAND, A. R. AND BURKE, R. S. A Measurement of Sociability. *Journal of Applied Psychology,* 1926, 10, 315–326.

31. HALL, L. K. *The 1926–1927 Character Growth Tests of the Y.M.C.A.* Unpublished report.

32. HARTMAN, ROSS AND DASHIELL, J. F. An Experiment to Determine the Relation of Interests to Abilities. *Psychological Bulletin,* 1919, 16, 259–262.

33. HARTSHORNE, HUGH AND MAY, MARK A. *Testing the Knowledge of Right and Wrong.* Religious Education Association, Monograph Number 1, 1927. Pp. 72.

34. HEIDBREDER, EDNA. Measuring Introversion and Extroversion. *Journal of Abnormal and Social Psychology,* 1926, 21, 120–134.

35. HEIDBREDER, EDNA. The Normal Inferiority Complex. *Journal of Abnormal and Social Psychology,* 1927, 22, 243–258.

36. HOLLINGWORTH, H. L. *Judging Human Character.* New York: D. Appleton and Company, 1922. Pp. xiii, 268.

37. HUBBARD, R. M. Interests Studied Quantitatively. *Journal of Personnel Research,* 1926, 4, 365–378.

38. HUBBARD, R. M. The Reliability of Freyd's Interest Analysis Blank. *Journal of Educational Psychology,* 1926, 17, 617–624.

39. HUGHES, W. H. A Rating Scale for Individual Capacities, Attitudes, and Interests. *Journal of Educational Method,* 1923, 3, 56–65.

40. HULL, CLARK L. *Aptitude Testing.* Yonkers, N. Y.: World Book Company, 1928. Pp. xvi, 536.

41. JOHNSTON, J. B. Predicting Success or Failure in College at the Time of Entrance. *School and Society,* 1924, 19, 772.

42. JOHNSTON, J. B.   Predicting Success in College at the Time of Entrance. *School and Society*, 1926, 23, 82–88.

43. JONES, E. S.   The Opinions of College Students.   *Journal of Applied Psychology*, 1926, 10, 427–436.

44. KELLEY, T. L.   *Interpretation of Educational Measurements*.   Yonkers, N. Y.: World Book Company, 1927.   Pp. xiv, 363.

45. KNIGHT, F. B.   The Significance of Unwillingness to be Tested.   *Journal of Applied Psychology*, 1922, 6, 211–212.

46. KNIGHT, F. B. AND FRANZEN, RAYMOND.   Pitfalls in Rating Schemes.   *Journal of Educational Psychology*, 1922, 6, 204–212.

47. KORNHAUSER, A. W.   Results from a Quantitative Questionnaire on Likes and Dislikes Used with a Group of College Freshmen.   *Journal of Applied Psychology*, 1927, 11, 85–95.

48. KRIEGER, LAURA.   *Prediction of Success in Professional Courses for Teachers*. Contributions to Education, Number 420, Teachers College, New York, 1930. Pp. 77

49. LAIRD, D. A.   How Personalities are Found in Industry.   *Industrial Psychology*, 1926, 1, 654–662.

50. LUNDBERG, G. A.   Sex Differences on Social Questions.   *School and Society*, 1926, 23, 595–600.

51. MANSON, GRACE E.   *Bibliography on Psychological Tests and Other Objective Measures in Industrial Personnel*.   Reprint and Circular Series, Personnel Research Federation, 4.   Pp. 28.   Also in *Journal of Personnel Research*, 1925, 4, 301–328.

52. MANSON, GRACE E.   *Bibliography of the Analysis and Measurement of Human Personality up to 1926*.   Reprint and Circular Series, National Research Council, Number 72.   Pp. 59.

53. MARSH, S. E. AND PERRIN, F. A. C.   An Experimental Study of the Rating Scale Technique.   *Journal of Abnormal and Social Psychology*, 1925, 19, 383–399.

54. MARSTON, L. R.   *Emotions of Young Children; an Experimental Study in Introversion and Extroversion*.   Studies in Child Welfare, 3; First Series, Number 95; University of Iowa, 1925.   Pp. 99.

55. MAY, MARK A.   Predicting Academic Success.   *Journal of Educational Psychology*, 1923, 14, 429–440.

56. MAY, MARK A. AND HARTSHORNE, HUGH.   Personality and Character Tests. *Psychological Bulletin*, 1926, 23, 395–411; 1927, 24, 418–435.

57. MAY, M. A., HARTSHORNE, H., AND WELTY, R. E.   Personality and Character Tests.   *Psychological Bulletin*, 1928, 25, 422–443; 1929, 26, 418–444.

58. MAY, MARK A. AND HARTSHORNE, HUGH.   *Studies in Deceit*.   Book I, *General Methods and Results;*   Book II, *Statistical Methods and Results*.   New York: Macmillan Company, 1928.   Pp. xxi, 414; viii, 306.

59. MINER, J. B.   The Evaluation of a Method for Finely Graduated Estimates of Abilities.   *Journal of Applied Psychology*, 1917, 1, 123–135.

60. MINER, J. B.   An Analysis of Vocational Interests.   *School Review*, 1925, 23, 744–754.

61. MORRIS, ELIZABETH H.   *Personal Traits and Success in Teaching*.   Contributions to Education, Number 342, Teachers College, 1929.   Pp. 75.

62. MORRIS, ELIZABETH H. *Teachers Handbook for Morris Trait Index L.* Bloomington, Ill.: Public School Publishing Company, 1929. Pp. 7.

63. MOSS, F. A. AND HUNT, T. Ability to Get Along with Others. *Industrial Psychology*, 1926, 1, 170–178.

64. NEWCOMB, T. N. *The Consistency of Certain Extrovert-Introvert Behavior Patterns of Fifty-one Problem Boys.* Contributions to Education, Number 382, Teachers College, 1929. Pp. 123.

65. ODELL, C. W. *Predicting the Scholastic Success of College Freshmen.* Bureau of Educational Research, University of Illinois, Bulletin Number 37, 1927. Pp. 54.

66. ROBACK, A. A. *A Bibliography of Character and Personality.* Cambridge: Science-Art Publishers, 1927. Pp. 340.

67. ROGERS, A. L. Mental Tests for the Selection of University Students. *British Journal of Psychology, General Section*, 1925, 15, 405–415.

68. ROSENOW, CURT. Predicting Academic Achievement. *Pedagogical Seminary*, 1925, 32, 628–636.

69. RUGG, HAROLD. Is the Rating of Human Character Practicable? *Journal of Educational Psychology*, 1921, 12, 425–438; 485–501. 1922, 13, 30–42; 81–93.

70. RUGG, HAROLD. *A Primer of Graphics and Statistics.* Boston: Houghton Mifflin Company, 1925. Pp. 139.

71. SCHWEGLER, R. A. *A Study of Introvert-Extravert Responses to Certain Test Situations.* Contributions to Education, Number 361, Teachers College, 1929.

72. SHUTTLEWORTH, FRANK K. *The Measurement of the Character and Environmental Factors Involved in Scholastic Success.* University of Iowa Studies: Studies in Character, 1, Number 2, 1927. Pp. 80.

73. SHUTTLEWORTH, FRANK K. Environmental and Character Factors Involved in Scholastic Success: 1926–1927 Data. *Journal of Educational Psychology*, 1929, 20, 424–433.

74. SLAGHT, W. E. *A Study of Truthfulness in Children.* Iowa Studies in Character, Number 4. University of Iowa.

75. SPENCE, RALPH B. *The Improvement of College Marking Systems.* Contributions to Education, Number 252, Teachers College, 1927. Pp. vi, 89.

76. STRONG, E. K., JR. Interests Analysis of Personnel Managers. *Journal of Personnel Research*, 1926, 5, 235–242.

77. STRONG, E. K., JR. An Interest Test for Personnel Managers. *Journal of Personnel Research*, 1926, 5, 194–203.

78. STRONG, E. K., JR. Vocational Guidance of Executives. *Journal of Applied Psychology*, 1927, 11, 331–347.

79. SWEET, LENNIG. *Measurement of Personal Attitudes in Younger Boys.* Occasional Studies, Number 9. New York: Association Press, 1929. Pp. 57.

80. THORNDIKE, E. L. Permanence of Interests and Their Relation to Abilities. *Popular Science Monthly*, 1912, 81, 449–456.

81. THORNDIKE, E. L. The Correlation Between Interests and Abilities in College Courses. *Psychological Review*, 1921, 28, 374–376.

82. THURSTONE, L. L. Predictive Value of Mental Tests. *Educational Review*, 1922, 63, 11–22.

83. TOOPS, H. A. AND SYMONDS, P. M. What Shall We Expect of the A.Q.? *Journal of Educational Psychology*, 1922, 13, 513–528; 1923, 14, 27–38.

84. TRAVIS, R. C. The Measurement of Fundamental Character Traits by a New Diagnostic Test. *Journal of Abnormal and Social Psychology*, 1925, 19, 400–420.

85. TROW, W. C. *The Psychology of Confidence*. Archives of Psychology, Number 67, 1923.

86. UHRBROCK, R. S. Interest as an Indication of Ability. *Journal of Applied Psychology*, 1926, 10, 487–501.

87. UHRBROCK, R. S. Personal Estimates of Character Traits. *Pedagogical Seminary*, 1926, 33, 491–496.

88. VOELKER, PAUL. *The Functions of Ideals and Attitudes in Social Education*. Contributions to Education, Number 112, Teachers College, 1921. Pp. 126.

89. WATSON, G. B. *The Measurement of Fair Mindedness*. Contributions to Education, Number 176, Teachers College, 1925. Pp. 97.

90. WATSON, G. B. Character Tests of 1926. *Vocational Guidance Magazine*, 1927, 5, 289–309.

91. WATSON, G. B. AND BIDDLE, DELIA H. *A Year of Research—1927*. Religious Education Association, Monograph Number 4, 1929. Pp. v, 82.

92. WATSON, G. B. AND CHASSELL, JOSEPH O. *The Emotional History Record*. October, 1925 Revision. Unpublished.

93. WELLS, F. L. Report on a Questionnaire Study of Personality Traits with a College Graduate Group. *Mental Hygiene*, 1925, 9, 113–127.

94. YOAKUM, C. S. AND MANSON, GRACE E. Self Ratings as a Means of Determining Trait-Relationships and Relative Desirability of Traits. *Journal of Abnormal and Social Psychology*, 1926, 21, 52–64.

95. YULE, G. UDNY. *An Introduction to the Theory of Statistics*. London: Charles Griffin and Company, 1927. Pp. xv, 422.